Crockett's Long Trip To Kentucky

Colonel Charles Dahnmon Whitt

Taken from the Novel, "Legacy 2nd Edition, The Days Of David Crockett Whitt"
Published by Dahnmon Whitt Family Publishing
P. O. Office Box 831
Flatwoods, KY 41139
Phone 606 836 7997
Cell 606 571 1820
E-Mail c-dahnmon@roadrunner.com
Web-site http://dahnmonwhittfamily.com

Published January 2014

All rights reserved, Copy-write by Dahnmon Whitt Family Publishing
No part of this book may be reproduced by any manner or method with our written Permission by the Publisher. Furthermore it cannot be utilized in any form or movie, or on film!

ISBN 978-1-63068-240-8

Crockett's Long Trip To Kentucky

Preface

One day, in the hills of Montgomery County Virginia, a baby was born. This day was December 13, 1836, the same year that the Alamo fell. Some famous American died at the battle of the Alamo. Jonas and Susannah Whitt, the father and mother of this new baby were well aware of this famous American. They would name their baby after the brave man who died at the Alamo. This new little person will be known from then on as David Crockett Whitt.

This collection of information will be about David Crockett Whitt and his family, his travels, his hard times, and his adventures. I will be as accurate as possible, but I will add my thoughts to fill in missing information. This will be history with a little fiction mingled in to keep you awake.

Hezekiah and Rachel were the parents of Jonas Whitt and the grandparents of David Crockett Whitt.

After Jonas lost his wife, mother, and father, he got restless feet and was ready to move to the west. When he got word to come to Kentucky to build a grist-mill, he and young Crockett headed to Greenup County, Kentucky to build a grist mill. (Some 200 miles through rugged terrain)

This is a day to day saga of Crockett Whitt and his link to Kentucky. Travel with him and Jonas to see what they will do next.

Crockett's Long Trip To Kentucky

Contents

Chapter		Page
1	Crockett Will See Kentucky	3
2	Head Of The River	21
3	Kentucky Border	40
4	Follow The Levisa	62
5	Heading For The Ohio	90
6	Let's Go Build A Mill	104
7	Building A Mill In Truittville	123
8	Jonas Falls In Love	142
9	Order Is In, Get Back To Millie	170
10	Hannah's Coming To Kentucky	184
11	Jonas Takes A Bride	196
12	Marriages and Discord	210
13	Salvation and Trouble On The Tug Fork	226
14	About The Author	244

Crockett's Long Trip To Kentucky

Chapter 1
Crockett will see Kentucky

Rachel seems about the same, she still speaks to Hezekiah as if he never died. She missed her children after they left for home.

The 20th of June Rachel did not eat a thing. She was so weak she could hardly turn over.

As evening came to Hezekiah Whitt House, Rachel summoned her family around her. She spoke in whispers, and eye gestures, portraying her love for each family member. She said that she could see a beautiful river and Hezekiah and Jesus were waiting for her. There were so many beautiful trees and flowers. Angels were abounding!

"Children, I am going home!" she said.

Rachel slipped off into a coma. Her body was shutting down, and her legs and arms were as cold as winter.

Nancy asked us to gather around and sing some hymns.

"Rachel will be able to hear us," she said.

James got a song book, and lined each verse, then the whole family sang the song verse by verse. This went on for about an hour, and then Rachel smiled and gave up the ghost. Jonas went to the clock and stopped it at 11:11 PM.

The family made tentative plans. Different ones would set up with their beloved mother through the night; Word would go out early in the morning so that final plans could be made. Jonas and James would take the first three hours of watch. Later others would be awakened to come and sit with the beloved Rachel. First light the ladies would come and bath Rachel and put her in a favorite dress. A coffin was already prepared, because of recent events. Jonas and James had worked on the coffin with love.

As Jonas and James sat and talked in the bedroom. They had reflected on all that had gone on since their Paw died. They begin to talk about Rachel seeing Hezekiah, and seeing the realms of glory.

"I think it is because of the Indian blood that flowed through her veins, you know that she is the Daughter of the great Chief Cornstalk" James said.

"That explains it, I bout forgot about her father being Cornstalk. I have always heard that Indians have an inside line to the spirit world." Jonas said.

"Me too," replied James.

"Bless her heart, she and Paw can go on to glory now," exclaimed Jonas.

Jonas described how they both lived long, productive lives. They were great examples of how we should live and treat our fellowmen. They both had great faith in Jesus, and the promise of heaven.

Next morning James Griffith and David Crockett rode out in different directions to let the folks know that Rachel had passed. In a short time people started showing up with food and offering to help in any way possible.

Elder David Young was one of the first to show up. He wanted to get there to offer spiritual guidance and console the family. Five more men showed up with picks and shovels to prepare the grave. One of the men made a mistake by asking where she would be buried.

Jonas rose up in anger, "what do you mean?"

"Sorry Jonas, but your mother was Indian wasn't she?"

"She will be buried beside her lifelong friend and husband," commanded Jonas.

"Do not come in here with that Indian race stuff," Jonas said.

"Sorry Jonas I was only going with what folks sometimes do," answered the neighbor.

Jonas patted him on the back, "thanks Frank for coming over to help," Jonas said.

Crockett's Long Trip To Kentucky

"Maw will be buried right beside of Paw, any one comes to stop you, you send them to me," said Jonas.

"Yes sir, I understand," answered Frank.

There would be a wake the night of the 21st. and the funeral would be at noon on the 22nd. This has been a hard year for the Whitt's with both Hezekiah and Rachel passing away. People in Tazewell County are so kind and caring in these times, Jonas thought.

Hezekiah was well known and so was his loving wife, Rachel Whitt. Hezekiah was always ready to extend a hand to any one that needed help. Hezekiah was especially helpful in legal matters and in politics. Rachel was just a grand neighbor to everyone.

Large crowds came to pay honor to Rachel at her wake. Some came only to have a short visit, while others would sit out the night with the Whitt family. Some folks didn't even know Rachel personally, but knew of her good deeds and of her prominent husband.

Some of the family would hide out for a nap. Some of the family was always vigil for the entire wake. There was much conversation and well wishing to the family. Many stories were told about Rachel, and of course Hezekiah.

Crockett stayed around the wake until Jonas sent him to bed. Jonas told him that the family wanted him to lead the procession tomorrow. I think it will be fine to carry the old flag one more time, since it belonged to Grand Maw now.

The coffin was really nice. The sons had fashioned it out of wild cherry wood. Crockett had helped with the sanding and rubbing in of the bee wax. It was a fitting coffin for any high ranking person. Rachel was the highest ranking Matriarch of the Whitt clan. When Hezekiah and Rachel passed away a whole social and historic realm passed from existence. They would be sorely missed by family and friends.

At about 11:40 A.M., Jonas instructed Crockett to take the old war flag and start the line. The coffin carried by six strong friends was next, followed by James and Nancy. The rest of the brothers and sisters were next; followed by all the

Crockett's Long Trip To Kentucky

remaining family. Then the many friends followed up the procession in the rear. As the line moved down the hill and crossed Green Mountain Road, many other people joined in at the rear. Many people showed up for the funeral, but not quite the crowd that honored Hezekiah a couple months back.

Like before Crockett carried the old flag high and proud at a slow respectful pace.

At the top of the hill the Elder David Young and most of the Baptist congregation were waiting. Crockett stepped aside as the men set the coffin on timbers that lay across the open grave. The family came around and took a seat on the benches in front of the grave. Crockett draped the flag across the cherry wood coffin, and took a seat beside his Paw.

The Elder took over the service, and preached a great sermon, many hymns were sung. The Elder also told of recent events of Rachel seeing Hezekiah and Jesus waiting for her. She had no dread of death because she knew beyond a shadow of doubt that heaven was hers.

"This even in death was a great witness for the Lord Jesus Christ," The Elder added.

After, the funeral people came by to shake hands with the family and offer one last condolence. The skies had been gray all morning. Now the rain began with a mist at first. In a short period the rain became heavy. The grave was almost covered by the time the heavy rain came.

Crockett quoted the saying he heard Jonas say about two months back, "Happy the dead the rains falls up on, happy the bride the sun shines up on"

Jonas heard this and turned to Crockett and said, "That is a good saying son."

"It seems to always rain on the funeral of good folks," James said.

The family gathered in at the Hezekiah Whitt House. After more eating and visiting, the family began to disperse.

Everyone knew the wishes of Hezekiah and Rachel as to the house and farm. It was to go to the oldest son James. James and Nancy had moved in over a year

Crockett's Long Trip To Kentucky

ago to care for the elderly parents. No one would object to this. There was several other farms and acreage's to be dispersed at a later time.

Late that evening, as Jonas, James Griffith, and Crockett sat and reflected on the day's events. Jonas right out of the blue said, "I am going to Kentucky, you fellers in favor?"

Crockett spoke right up, "I am Paw."

"I don't want to right now, me and Nancy Webb are getting close, I will stay and take care of the farm if that is alright," James Griffith stated.

Jonas answered James, "You are a man now son and I respect your decision."

"We will start planning tomorrow, Hannah has pretty much adopted James and Nancy, she is too young to go off on a sashay like this, she will be better off with Nancy," Jonas said.

"We will go and build Sam a mill or two, if we would decide to stay we will come back and get the little darling," Jonas continued..

"Looks like just you and me Crockett, do you want to build some mills in Greenup County, Kentucky," asked Jonas?
"Yes sir, I will be a big help Paw," replied Crockett.

The very next morning Jonas wrote a letter to Doctor Samuel Truitt, Truittville Post Office, Greenup County, Kentucky. He stated that he would be available to come and build the two mills on contract. Jonas stated that he would leave the next day after a reply. He also stated what compensation he would expect including room and board for him and his ten year old son.

"Crockett," Jonas called out, "here son, watch for the postman and get this in the outgoing mail."
"Do not lose it if you want to go to Kentucky," Jonas added.

"I won't Paw, I will put it in the Postman's hand," answered Crockett.

Crockett headed out on this very important errand.

Crockett's Long Trip To Kentucky

"Wonder how long we will have to wait for an answer Paw?" Crockett asked as soon as he got back.

"I figure around the end of August, now Crockett don't get disappointed if the Truitt's don't need us anymore," said Jonas.

"He may have found a millwright by now," added Jonas.

"Alright Paw, I bet we get a reply in August," exclaimed Crockett.

"Hope you are right son," answered Jonas.

"In the mean time we have much to do, we got crops to take care of, and animals, and equipment to make ready," said Jonas.

"We will take a wagon, and all my tools, we will have to do some planning, for the harvest, and sell some things," Jonas continued.

"We have plenty to do, but plenty of time to do it, I think," said Jonas.

Things got back to almost normal. Jonas made plans to wait until the spring of 1847 to head to Kentucky, if Doctor Samuel Truitt confirmed the agreement. This way there would be no haste in getting ready. The crops could be harvested, and everyone could have ample time to say their good byes.

Crockett was a little disappointed; He wanted to head right out.

The whole country was excited about the western lands. James Polk was President during this time, and he pushed for expansion of the United States. He had settled a dispute with Great Britain, and established the border on the 49th parallel between Canada and the United States. Also, he offered to buy California and New Mexico from Mexico for Twenty Million Dollars. The Mexican government did not have power to sell off half of its lands so nothing was settled.

General Zachary Taylor was sent to the Rio Grande with troops. The Mexicans attacked which started a shooting war. The United States soon defeated the Mexicans in several battles. The United States took over California and New

Crockett's Long Trip To Kentucky

Mexico and gave the Mexican Government Fifteen Million Dollars for damages. New territories brought on a new problem with the state of slavery. That's another thing for the North and South to disagree about. Expansion was in the air and many people picked up and headed toward the west. It is no wonder that Jonas got itchy feet.

The first week of September, a letter arrived for Jonas Whitt. Crockett got the mail that day. He saw the return address and was filled with excitement.

He ran to Jonas with the letter saying, "It's here Paw."

Jonas took the letter and with his pocket knife, slowly opened the envelope. Crockett was about to pass out with anticipation. Finally Jonas removed the letter, unfolded its pages and begins to read.

Dear Mister Jonas Whitt, I received your letter and am delighted that you are available to come and build my grist mill. I do approve your statement of compensation and room and board. I have an Inn, and you and your son will be quiet comfortable for your extended stay in Kentucky.

Please send me a conformation as to when you may arrive here in Greenup, County Kentucky. Your Humble Servant, Doctor Samuel Truitt.

"Yea, yea," shouted Crockett, "we are going to Kentucky!"

"Looks that way," replied Jonas.

I will write him a letter today and mail it tomorrow. We will leave about the end of March 1847, and we will need detailed directions to Big White Oak Creek in Greenup County.

"Why can't we go now paw?" asked Crockett.

"It is so long until next March!" Crockett added.

Jonas explained that it would be better not to be hasty, a well planned trip will be much better. We have a lot of things to finish here. March will be here before you know it. Our tools will have to be cleaned and oiled. The wagon will have to be

Crockett's Long Trip To Kentucky

put in top notch shape. Axles will have to be greased and all the harness gear will have to be gone over. Kentucky is a long hard trip. We sure don't want to have a break down on the trail.

Jonas went on explaining about how much there was to do here on the farm. We will have time to sell the tobacco and other crops.

You have wood to chop for the winter, and plenty of other things to keep you busy. We may even have time to go fishing a time or two before it turns cold.

"What about hunting this winter," ask Crockett?

"We should be able to get out and maybe get a deer or turkey for the table," answered Jonas.

Jonas and Crockett take almost daily walks to the cemetery to visit with Susannah, Hezekiah, and Rachel. Crockett can hardly remember his Maw, but he loves her very much because of all the stories about her. He has been making trips with Jonas to the cemetery for six or seven years. He remembers Grand Paw and Grand Maw very vividly, since he spent so much time with them.

Jonas and Crockett would always stop at the old Hezekiah Whitt house on the way home. Jonas told Crockett that they would have to start calling the old house the James Whitt house.

Hannah loved her Paw but stayed with James and Nancy most of the time. Nancy had a way with children, even though she had none of her own.

James Griffith was still living with Crockett and their Paw Jonas. James Griffith was a full grown man now at twenty one years old. He was the main work hand on the Indian Creek farm, but spends much time in Jeffersonville.

He has become very popular with the young ladies of Tazewell County. He has one young lady that is the object of his affection, Nancy Webb. She is still too young to have a full time beau; at least her Paw Joseph Webb has confirmed to James Griffith Whitt.

When Jonas and Crockett leave in the spring, James Griffith will stay and run the

Crockett's Long Trip To Kentucky

Indian Creek Farm. Hannah will stay with James and Nancy while Jonas is away in Kentucky. If by chance Jonas and Crockett decide to stay in Kentucky, Jonas will come for Hannah, and the farm will be sold. But that is a long time off, and "we live here for now," said Jonas to Crockett.

"Paw do you think we may stay in Kentucky?" asked Crockett.

"Don't know son, but we will be there for a long time building two mills," replied Jonas.

"Who knows we may get even more work to do after we get there," Jonas added.

All through the fall and winter Jonas kept his sons busy with the farm work and preparation for the spring trip. Jonas also made visits to all of his children on every opportunity. Also the children spent time with them at the Indian Creek Farm. Good memories were made and would have to last until Jonas and Crockett returned from Kentucky.
Just before Christmas, the thirteenth of December, Crockett's eleventh birthday a letter arrived from Kentucky. It was the letter they had been waiting for. It was from Doctor Samuel Truitt, with detailed directions to the Truitt property in Greenup County.

This was as good a Christmas and birthday present to Crockett as he could wish for. He had never been on a long trip since the family came from Montgomery County back in 1837. It really seems true now that this letter has arrived.

James Griffith and Crockett went on several hunting trips that winter. Crockett had sharpened up his hunting and shooting skills. He was tall for his age and quiet strong. Jonas told them if they didn't quit carrying in game there would be too much to handle. And besides that they better leave a few critters in the woods for the future. James Griffith and Crockett had a good laugh over that.

It was the first of March 1847 and final plans were made for the trip. Jonas wanted to stop and see his brother John Bunyon in Floyd County, on the way. They would be able to have a short visit and get some rest. By then a good home cooked meal will be a good diversion from the trail cuisine.

Getting there they would follow the Kentucky Turnpike that runs by Indian Creek

Crockett's Long Trip To Kentucky

Farm. They would follow the road through Indian, (now Cedar Bluff) north west to a bottom called Richlands. Then they would continue to a place now called (Raven). Here they would leave the Clinch Valley to climb to the top of a long ridge. (Now Road Ridge) They would ramble along this ridge for several miles and finally descend to a little valley.

The ridge is a divide for the water shed. Water on one end takes a southern flow. Water on the other end takes a north western flow. This little valley had a small creek winding North West beginning at the bottom of the ridge. This creek is a fork of the Big Sandy River. The Creek is called Louisa Creek (now Levisa) some folks call this area "Head of the River". The terrain would change drastically.

The mountains close in on the trail. They would follow the Levisa Fork to the Big Sandy River which begins at the confluence of the Tug Fork. The valley is very narrow.

Finally the end of March arrived, and the trip would begin. April is unpredictable in this part of the country, so heavy coats and light coats would both be on hand.

"I just hope we don't get caught in a snow storm," Jonas said.

One thing about it, they don't usually last long in April," Jonas added.

"I remember a few years back we got a foot of snow, remember Paw," exclaimed James Griffith?

"Yes I do, we have a good tent and provisions, so we can weather a snow for a day or two," Jonas said.

The wagon was packed with care and everything tied down and covered. The best team of Mules was hitched to the wagon. Jonas' saddle horse Jake was tied to the back of the wagon. He would be a spare if something happened to one the mules. After their arrival Jake would be the transportation around Greenup County. A rifle, shotgun, and Jonas' cap and ball pistol would be handy as well. The basket of fried chicken and other food items prepared by the women was sat on the floor under the seat. A small barrel of water was also part of the load.

Every one of Jonas' children was on hand that morning to see them off. Jonas and

Crockett's Long Trip To Kentucky

Crockett hugged each loved one, and got up in the wagon. This day was the twenty eighth of March 1847. Jonas and Crockett pulled out on the Kentucky Turnpike and headed toward Kentucky. It was about twenty minutes past eight A.M.

Jonas and Crockett bounced along the road toward Indian. (Now Cedar Bluff) Crockett said to Jonas, "I didn't think we would ever finally get started to Kentucky."

"Well son" replied Jonas, "you are starting to learn patience."

"Now you have an adventure ahead of you, but a long hard trip also," Jonas said.

Jonas explained that they need to take their time, because they have a heavy load, and the road down Levisa Fork is rough and narrow.

"I was over that way awhile back," Jonas said.

"I was over there checking on the farm for Paw; He had it rented out," said Jonas.

"It is located on Dismal Creek and Levisa Fork; (Now Buchanan, County) and that is as far as I have been in that direction," Jonas added.

"I remember Paw, you stayed overnight and you were riding Jake," Crockett replied.

"That is right, and you know Jake makes good time," Jonas said.

"We may get a third way there today with this wagon," Jonas added.

"Well where we get is where we get," answered Crockett.

"That's right son, be patient," Jonas said.

As Crockett drove the wagon through the village of Indian, Jonas waved to the folks.

"We know most of these people don't we Paw?" asked Crockett.

Crockett's Long Trip To Kentucky

"Yes and most of them know we are heading for Kentucky," Jonas exclaimed.

The weather was not bad, but the March wind had not gone away. The grass was green, and the trees wanted to burst out in bloom. Jonas was whistling a tune and the two were quite happy. They followed the Turnpike south west along the Clinch River. Before long the valley widened out into a big bottom. The ground was rich and folks had a big portion plowed under in anticipation of spring planting.

There was a village here also; some folks called it Town Hill. Some folks called it the most likely name, Rich-lands.

"Paw," asked Crockett, "why do folks call this place Town Hill?" asked Crockett.

Jonas gets out a piece of chicken and a biscuit nods to Crockett, chicken son?
    Crockett nods back with a yes answer. Jonas looks to the right at a knoll overlooking the valley.

"Up there son, they say the Indians had a town there once up on a time," Jonas said.

At the western end of this beautiful valley they stopped at a creek.

"This is Hill Creek son, we better water our mules and Jake," Jonas instructed.

"We can stretch our legs a bit too," Jonas added.

Crockett drove the wagon into the creek, stopping with the mules standing in the water. Jonas untied Jake and took him to water also. After watering the animals the trip was resumed.

They followed the old Turn Pike hugging the North side of the hills.

"We will be getting to where we start our climb up the Turnpike Ridge before long," Jonas said.

Jonas explained that the Turnpike traveled the ridge for a number of miles, and

Crockett's Long Trip To Kentucky

hopefully we will get a good start on it today.

They stopped at another creek (now Coal Creek) and watered the mules again. Jonas explained that the mules don't need watered very badly, but it may be the last they get for a while." (This place is the present town of Raven.)

The basket was a joy for the two to snack on as they traveled.

"We will not have to do any cooking this evening will we paw?" Crockett asked.

"Not much," answered Jonas.
　　"It is a pity we will not have a full basket fixed for us every day," Crockett said.

"Yes," said Jonas, "we could head back to Indian Creek and get one for tomorrow."

Crockett laughed, "That's alright Paw, we can do without it."

"Now get ready to do some climbing son, head right up this grade, we are starting the climb up Turnpike Ridge," Jonas said. (Now Road Ridge)

Crockett headed the mules up the grade at a nice slow pace.

"That's right son, don't push them too hard," Jonas said.

Jonas mentioned that they were going to leave the Clinch Valley. Right down the river from here is a creek called Mill Creek. There is a Grist Mill up the creek a-ways, at a beautiful falls.

"I worked over there a day or two for the folks doing some repairs, sometime back," explained Jonas.

"Who was it that owned it Paw," asked Crockett?

"Don't remember, but it was something like Stinson," Jonas replied.

At the top of the first hill the road continued on up the Ridge. The road took a westerly direction. The two looked back over the Clinch Valley. They could see a

Crockett's Long Trip To Kentucky

big mountain that followed the river, and ran for miles.
"Look son this will be the last time you see Clinch Mountain for a spell," said Jonas.

"It is a beautiful place ain't it Paw!" said Crockett.

"Yes it is son, but we will see some beautiful grounds in the Kentucky lands, exclaimed Jonas.

"Want me to drive for a while son?" asked Jonas.

"No Paw I got it, unless you are getting a little afraid going up this steep ridge," answered Crockett.

"You are doing fine, just let the mules make their own pace," instructed Jonas.

"I will paw," Crockett responded.

"Thank goodness this road levels off every now and then, to give the team a little break," Crockett said.

"Yes son," agreed Jonas "we will get to the summit and stop a little early for the night"

"The mules will need some rest after this pull," Jonas added.

About five that evening Jonas saw a good place to pull off and set up for the night. They un-hitched the team and scotched the wagon so it would not run off.

Jonas said to Crockett, "gather fire wood son, I am going to scout around for some water, I will be back dreckly."

"Alright Paw, I will, and I will start a fire." replied Crockett.

Jonas pointed to a rock house (overhanging cliff), "over there will be a good place," he said.

Crockett nodded, and Jonas was over the hill and out of site.

Crockett's Long Trip To Kentucky

In about an hour's time Jonas was back to camp.

Found some water, "I will take Jake, and the mules to water them," said Jonas.

"It is not far from here, you go ahead and start setting up camp," added Jonas.

"I will paw," answered Crockett, "that rock house will feel good tonight against this wind."

"Yelp, it is pretty breezy up here on this ridge," answered Jonas as he led the animals to water.

About an hour passed before Jonas was back.

"What took so long Paw, thought you said the water was close?" asked Crockett.

Jonas explained that it was close, but it is a small spring, they had to drink one at a time. Jonas put the feed bags on the animals, which held Oats. After supper we can hobble them and let them graze. This new grass will finish filling them up.

"The oats really give them energy, don't they Paw?" replied Crockett.

"Yes son, you have to take good care of your horses and mules, if you want them to take care of you!" replied Jonas.

After supper the two sit back by the fire and talked about the trip and many other things. Jonas told Crockett to keep the shotgun loaded and handy the rest of the way. There are bad men that prey upon the travelers in the Kentucky hills. Some of these bad men are here because they are wanted in the east or in central Kentucky. There is an old saying about this. If the law gets after you "head for the hills."

"We are in those hills son," said Jonas.
    Jonas told Crockett about the trip from Montgomery County to Tazewell County. His older brothers and sisters helped him hold off three bad men over in Rocky Gap.

Crockett's Long Trip To Kentucky

"I remember that story," replied Crockett.

"I was a baby and you all made the robbers back down with the old Brown Betsy's," replied Crockett.

"That is right, and I had a new 44 cap and ball revolver at that time, it is this same old pistol I carry when I'm out like this," said Jonas.
"Hope none of those bad fellers try to brother us Paw," said Crockett.

"Most likely they wouldn't son, just the same we will not let anyone get the jump on us," said Jonas.

"They would take everything we have and may be even kill us," replied Jonas.

Next morning the wind had laid down, but the temperature had dropped to an unpleasant level. Jonas got out from under his heavy quilts first and got the fire going. The rock house and fire made a pleasant place to sleep. Crockett got up and helped Jonas make ready for the days travel. After some hot breakfast, the two packed their gear back on the wagon. The mules were brought back and hitched to the wagon. Jake was tied to the back of the wagon and they were moving toward Kentucky once again.

They wore their heavy coats today, the temperature was slow to rise and the wind begins to pick up again. As they rode along, Jonas told Crockett that they may make it over to Grand Paw's property on Dismal Creek and Levisa Fork today.

"Who lives there Paw," asked Crockett?

"A Mister James Thompson rents the place," replied Jonas.

"He seemed interested in buying it the last time I talked to him," said Jonas.

"When your Uncle James probates the will for your Grand Paw and Grand Maw, it will be sold; Mister Thompson may buy it;" said Jonas.

"How much land is it Paw," Crockett asked?

"It is pretty good size, about 245 acres I think," said Jonas.

Crockett's Long Trip To Kentucky

"Well at any rate that will be a good place to stop and water the team and take a rest, said Jonas.

"We might even be able to mooch a meal from the Thompson's," added Jonas.

"When will we get there Paw?" asked Crockett.

"Don't know, but it will be quite some time, we have to travel this ridge for several miles, then we have to go slow back down the other side of this ridge," explained Jonas.

As they rode along they passed, a wagon headed toward Tazewell County. A Mister Blankenship was taking a load of coal to the Perry family. They talked for a few minutes, and both wagons resumed their journey. Crockett wanted to know what the Perry's would do with coal.

"Burn it son," replied Jonas.

"It is much slower burning and puts out more heat than wood," Jonas said. "The Perry's are rich ain't they Paw?" asked Crockett.

"Well to do, you could say," Jonas replied.

Jonas and Crockett passed another wagon heading toward Kentucky, There was a whole family on this wagon and it was pulled by two yoke of oxen.

"The oxen are very strong, but not very fast," replied Jonas.

They talked with these folks for a few minutes also. They were out of Russell County, heading to a place called Lexington, Kentucky. This family was the Holbrook's.

"They wanted to start a new life in the blue grass lands," Mister Holbrook said.

Crockett said, "They have blue grass in Tazewell County."

Yes we heard that, but we want the flatter lands we have heard of in Kentucky," replied Mister Holbrook.

"We better get a going, we may see you later, take care!" said Jonas.

"You do the same," answered Mister Holbrook.

Crockett told Jonas, "That is the biggest wagon I ever seen."
"I know," Jonas replied, "they are going pretty slow because of the big load and size."

"That is the kind of wagons they use going across the prairie to Oregon," said Jonas.

"Tough going in this country," said Crockett.

Yes nodded Jonas and they moved on leaving the giant wagon behind.

Hezekiah Whitt Home
Baptist Valley, Tazewell County, VA

Crockett's Long Trip To Kentucky

Chapter 2
Head Of The River.

Jonas and Crockett continue out the ridge on the Kentucky Turnpike. They are getting close to the descent, and they will have to apply the brakes. A runaway wagon can bring death and destruction in a hurry. Jonas warned Crockett about the steep grade ahead!

"I am ready for the steep grade, I got my big foot right here on the brake Paw," said Crockett.

"Alright son, I just want you to be prepared," exclaimed Jonas.

As they went down the winding road Crockett said; "Paw my ears keep popping."

"That is normal son, we have gone downhill a long way; I think your ears have to adapt to the elevation," Jonas answered.

"Well ain't that something; I never thought of that," exclaimed Crockett.

Jonas started telling Crockett about the divide up on the ridge. He explained that the water shed is different over here on this side of the ridge.

"What do you mean Paw," asked Crockett?

"The Clinch River runs mostly south, and over here the water will run toward the northwest," Jonas said.

"When we get down to where we are beside the creek you will see what I mean," Jonas added.

Crockett drove the wagon like a teamster; he drove down that steep curvy road without any mishap. Before long they were riding on a slight downhill grade, almost level. The creek was on their right as the road meandered along beside it.

"Look at the creek, it is heading toward the north," Jonas said.
"Yes paw, is that Levisa Fork, asked Crockett?

Crockett's Long Trip To Kentucky

"It sure is, we are at the head of the river," Jonas answered.

"We can follow this water all the way to the Ohio River," replied Jonas.

"Wow Paw, this will help to keep us from getting lost." said Crockett.

Jonas laughingly said, "You are right about that!"
It is little right here, but the further we go the bigger it will become," said Jonas.

"The Russell Fork will hook up with it on down the river, right Paw," asked Crockett?

"That is right, it will become a river, even though it is a mere creek right here," said Jonas.

"Then way on down the Tug Fork will join in, from that point it is the Big Sandy River," Jonas added.

"Paw I know about the Tug, it is not too far from where we live in Tazewell County," answered Crockett.

"That's right son, over a few ridges and you are there at its head water," Jonas said.

"Why didn't we go that way to Kentucky, Paw?" Crockett asked.

"Well we could have, but it is too rough and a poor road; we could never get our wagon through that a way," exclaimed Jonas.
"
We could have even went on down southwest to Lee County, and from there, turn northwest through the Cumberland Gap, and went that way," Jonas said.

"Do they have a good road that way Paw?" asked Crockett.

"Think so, only thing, it is much further that way from Indian Creek Farm," said Jonas.

Crockett's Long Trip To Kentucky

"Probably add a month to the trip," added Jonas.

"There is even another way, through Wise County, you go through Pound Gap, but that is also far and rough," Jonas stated.

"Better water the team and take a little rest son, they didn't get much water yesterday," said Jonas.

"Alright Paw; do you see somewhere to pull into the creek?" asked Crockett.

"No son, just stop here and we will lead them to the water," Jonas answered.

"Paw," Crockett said.

"Yes son," answered Jonas.

"Reckon the mules and Jake are a wondering where we are headed?" Crockett asked.
"Don't know son, you think of the dankest things," Jonas said.

As Jonas and Crockett proceed down the little bumpy and rutty road Jonas pulls out a plug of tobacco. Jonas cuts himself a jaw filling hunk and puts it back on the right side of his jaw. Crockett looked as Jonas meticulously loaded his mouth with an enjoyable chew of home grown tobacco.

"Paw, how about me trying a little chew?" Crockett asked.

"Well son, you will get sick, do you want to get sick?" asked Jonas.

"No I don't want to get sick, but that stuff looks good," answered Crockett.

"It doesn't make you sick, Paw," Crockett added.

"Well I will give you a little bit, if you start getting sick spit it out, and do not swallow any of the juice," explained Jonas.

"Alright paw," Crockett said excitedly!

Crockett's Long Trip To Kentucky

Jonas handed him a small portion of the juicy stuff. Crockett shoved it back into his jaw like he had seen Jonas do.

"What now paw?" Crockett asked.

"Just hold it in your mouth, when you get juice spit it out," said Jonas.

It was not long until the whole bit of it spewed from Crockett's mouth. Jonas gave out a big Hee-Haw! Crockett looked at his Paw, as if to say how do you chew that stuff?

The little narrow valley was damp, and the road had sections of deep ruts.

Jonas laughed as he said sarcastically; "Choose your rut well, as you will be in it for several miles."

"Ain't it the truth Paw?" Crockett said laughing.

Jonas was looking at the land marks and trying to remember where the Dismal Creek was.

"I think the farm is just ahead around the next bend," said Jonas.

"Paw there ain't many folks live over this way," replied Crockett.

"That is right, they are spread out pretty thin," answered Jonas.
"People are isolated over in this country, you have to like it or you would get lonesome," Jonas said.

"Does Mister Thompson have a large family?" asked Crockett.

"Well I think I remember five or six children, they are all ages," Jonas answered.

As the wagon rounded the bend in the road, they could see a steady stream of smoke flowing towards the heavens.

"That smoke just beyond those trees has to be the cabin of the Thompson's," said Jonas.

Crockett's Long Trip To Kentucky

Crockett became a little excited at the thought of meeting this family, way out here!

In another one hundred yards voices could be heard and motion was detected from the Thompson family. Mister Thompson and an older son were using a cross cut saw, and another son was chopping up the sawed pieces. A small boy was running around chasing the chickens.

Mister Thompson turned to the child and said, "Willie, stop that or them chickens will never start laying."

A small girl was gliding around the yard in a graceful dance in her imaginary world.

The little dancing girl looked up and hollered," Paw, wagon's coming."

Mister Thompson looked quickly in the direction of Jonas and Crockett.

Jonas immediately raised his hand and waved to the Thompson's.

"Hello there Mister Thompson," he shouted out.

This put James Thompson at ease, and he waved back. Crockett pulled the wagon off to the side of the road and locked the brake. They both got down and walked toward the house as James Thompson met them with a hand shake.

"Jonas isn't it, Jonas Whitt?" asked James.

"Yes and you are James Thompson," said Jonas.

"That's right," James answered.

Jonas introduced David Crockett to James and the children that were out in the yard. By now Mandy the wife of James and her two teen aged daughters came out on the porch to see what was going on.

"Jonas and Crockett, this here is my wife Mandy, and my girls Mary Jane, and Virginia," said James.

Crockett's Long Trip To Kentucky

Jonas stepped up and tipped his hat to the ladies. Crockett did likewise.

Virginia seemed to be about Crockett's age and her dark eyes sparkled like stars toward Crockett.

Crockett was instantly "twitter patted!"

James asked right off, "How is your Paw and Maw doing?"

Jonas was taken back a little?

"I guess you haven't heard, both Hezekiah and Rachel have passed on to glory," said Jonas.

"Oh! I'm so sorry to hear that, we only communicate about once a year when we send the rent," replied James.

"We sent it by our friend Bill McGraw last fall and never heard anything back," James said.

"Bill had to go to Jeffersonville on business so we had him take it," said James. "I got a receipt signed by James Whitt I think, I wondered about that at the time," added James.

"He is the administrator of the estate, so that would be right," Jonas replied.

"Is this place going up for sale?" James asked right off.

"Most likely when the will is probated," answered Jonas.

"You still interested in buying it," Jonas asked?

"Sure am if the price is right," replied James.

"Well if I were you, I would write a letter to James and let him know that you are interested," Jonas said.

Crockett's Long Trip To Kentucky

"I will do just that, I'm sorry to talk business before we have fed you and young David, exclaimed James.

"By the way what are you all doing way out on this end of the county," James asked?
Crockett spoke up, "going to Kentucky to build a mill!"

Jonas turned and looked at Crockett as if to say, you are speaking out of turn.

"Well you fellers are on the right road!" James said.

Virginia was still there gawking at Crockett!

James looked at her and said, "Girl go tell your Maw to set two more plates for supper!"

"Yes paw," answered the young lady.

"David would you like to go with me?" Virginia asked.

Crockett looked at Jonas asking, "Well I guess it will be alright if James don't mind."

"It's alright I reckon, they may put him to work in there, I try to stay out of the females way," James said.

"I know what you mean," replied Jonas.

"I think I will unhitch my team and let them do a little grazing while we eat supper with you kind folks," said Jonas.

"That will be fine, the grass is getting up purty good," said James.

"I guess tomorrow is April, if I looked at the calendar right;" replied James Thompson.

"Yelp," Exclaimed Jonas, "spring is trying to spring. "

Crockett's Long Trip To Kentucky

After supper Jonas and James talked about the current events, and the subject of Kentucky came up. James told Jonas that several folks have come by here lately on their way to Kentucky.

I heard of some mischief a happening over where Levisa goes by Grapevine Mountain. That is close to where she runs into the Russell fork.

James told Jonas to be extra careful from here on out. People have been beat and robbed. Some were shot outright cause they would not give up their stuff.

"How big a gang is it?" asked Jonas?
"I heard it was different little gangs of two to four un-Godly men," said James.

"They come to the mountains to get away from the law, and then they go after the folks that may look like easy pickings," James added.

"Crockett and I will not be easy to get a jump on, I already trained the boy to be vigilant," said Jonas.

Crockett and Virginia were like peas and carrots, they talked and talked. Of course Crockett had to brag and look like the big man, and Virginia had to listen intently. This was Crockett's first puppy love, and it was a new feeling for Virginia.

Before long, time had slipped away.

"Would you and Crockett like to stay in the barn tonight, and get an early start in the morning?" James asked.

"Well it is late, if you don't mind I will take you up on it, besides that it looks like rain is about to set in," Jonas answered.

Crockett and Virginia were delighted to hear the news. They could spend a few more hours together.

James told Virginia she had chores to do.

"I got to take care of the team and Jake,"
Crockett stated.

Crockett's Long Trip To Kentucky

"I got an idea, you help me and I will help you," Virginia said.

James overheard this.

"That will be alright long as both of you get your work done," said James.

Jonas and James sat on the porch and had a smoke and a little snort of corn squeezins! They enjoyed the conversation until almost dark.

Virginia and Crockett were carrying quilts toward the barn.

"Well Jim thanks for your hospitality, think I will get ready to turn in" said Jonas.

"You are welcome Jonas, how about sending my little girl back to the house," James said.
"I will do that, and good night," answered Jonas.

When Jonas went in to the barn, Crockett and Virginia were in an embrace enjoying a big kiss!

"Hummmmm," said Jonas!

They jumped back like they had been shot.

"Virginia, your Paw said it is time to come in the house," Jonas exclaimed.
    "Thank you Mister Whitt," she shyly replied.

"See you in the morning David," Virginia said.

Crockett nodded, "see you in the morning."

During the night the rain started. Jonas thought to himself, good to be in the barn on a night like this! Sleep came and morning came early. Jonas nudged Crockett.

"Want to go to Kentucky?" he asked?

"Will we be there today Paw?" asked Crockett.

Crockett's Long Trip To Kentucky

"No but we will be a lot closer than we are now," and laughed!

"Not funny Paw," mumbled the sleepy Crockett.

Crockett hurriedly yanked on his bibs and ran to the family privy.

A knock was heard as the big barn door squeaked open. The young black haired Virginia came in.

"Mister Whitt, my Maw told me to go and fetch you and David for breakfast," Virginia said.

"Thank you Miss Virginia, we will be heading that way in just a few minutes," replied Jonas.

"Where is David?" she blurted out.
    "He went to the little house out back," grinned Jonas.

"Ohoooo I'm sorry, never thought of that," she said quietly.

"I will run back and tell Maw you all will be a coming soon," said Virginia.

Jonas thought to himself, these young ones have got it bad! Good thing we are leaving, or we would have to sit around the clock watch them! Jonas thought, they will forget each other in a few days, he hoped!

Jonas and Crockett enjoyed a big breakfast with the Thompson's and got back on the road. The rain had subsided, but the road would be a bit mushy today. Before Crockett and Jonas got up on the wagon they shook hands with all the Thompson's. The starry eyed Virginia grabbed Crockett and gave him a bear hug! Mandy smiled as she witnessed her daughter's expression of puppy love. Jonas also noticed this!
Now the Whitts were on the move again, heading toward the Kentucky border.

Crockett committed on how nice the Thompson's were.

"They are nice people, I hope they can buy the farm," Jonas said.

Crockett's Long Trip To Kentucky

"Me too, I want to visit them again," replied Crockett.

"Them or her?" asked Jonas.

Crockett turned his head quickly and smiled.

"All of them of course, but mostly Virginia," Crockett said.

"Ain't she great Paw," asked Crockett?

"I reckon she is," replied Jonas.

"Now keep your eyes on the road today, the ruts will be bad, and we have to watch out for any sign of trouble," Jonas instructed.

"I will," said Crockett as he drove the sluggish wagon down the rutty Turnpike.

Time seemed to fly by this morning, but the miles were going slowly. The heavy wagon was hard to pull in the mushy road, so Crockett did not push the mules too hard. About 1:00 PM, they stopped to give the team a rest.
This gave Jonas and Crockett a chance to get down and stretch. Crockett asked Jonas if he heard anything about the road condition ahead.

"Well, Mister Thompson said it was not too bad, far as he knew, he did say after a rain it would be soft and rutty," Jonas said.

"He was right about that," replied Crockett.

Mister Thompson told me the road would get higher on the hills as we go into Kentucky.

"They want the road out of the flood plain, the road should drain better if that is the case," Jonas said.

"I hope he is right," replied Crockett, "this is slow going in this mud."

"We have to be patient and not over work the team," said Jonas, as they boarded the wagon.

"Paw how far is it to the Russell Fork and Grapevine Mountain?" asked Crockett.
"I think about two more days the rate we are a-going," answered Jonas.

"But we have to be vigilant from here on out," said Jonas.

"Mountain outlaws can show up around the very next bend, and as I told you they will kill just to see what's under our canvas," Jonas continued.
"Paw I am trying my best to keep a sharp eye out, and the shotgun is right here between my legs," replied Crockett.

"That is what it takes," replied Jonas.

"Crockett if we are confronted, you will know the danger," said Jonas.

"If you feel that our lives are in danger, and you will know, shoot to kill," Jonas continued seriously.

The hair rose up on the back of Crockett's neck.

"I hope I will know, and I hope I can shoot," replied Crockett.

"Don't worry, Whitt men know these things, when they come," replied Jonas.

"Did you ever have to kill Paw?" asked Crockett"

"No, but I came close a few times," answered Jonas.

"Grand paw Hezekiah had to kill several men, He killed Tories, Cherokee, and Creek Indians, replied Jonas.

"Who was the Tories?" asked Crockett.

"They were people that would not sign the Patriot's Oath, they sided with the King, and killed a lot of their neighbors," answered Jonas.
"Paw had to fight against some of them as well as the Indians, he did not relish the idea of killing white men or even Indians, he hated the fact that he shed blood,

Crockett's Long Trip To Kentucky

even though it was them or him," said Jonas.

"He said it stays with a man, that bad feeling of taking a life," Jonas added.

Crockett said seriously, "I hope I never have to let go on another man."

"I do too son, but if you and your property are threatened, by outlaw or war, you will have a duty to pay," said Jonas.

"I understand," said Crockett, "I think I could do it, if I am forced into it."

About 6:00 PM, Crockett saw a wide meadow ahead. It was rare for the valley to be this wide in this area.

"Paw that looks like a good place to camp tonight, what do you think," asked Crockett?

"Pull off the road and let's have a look around," replied Jonas.

"What about up there in the edge of the woods?" asked Crockett.

"Header on up there son," replied Jonas.

Crockett drove the team to the upper side of the meadow near the woods. He locked the brake and both got down. Crockett moved the shot gun over to the edge of the wagon so it would be handy.

Jonas noticed this, and said, "Good idea son."

"I am going to get on Jake and ride up the trail a-ways," said Jonas.

"You go ahead and unhitch the team and lead them to the creek, take your shotgun with you." Jonas said.

"Are you going to scout out the road up ahead, Paw?" asked Crockett.

"Yes son, I want to know what lies ahead since we will be sleeping here tonight," answered Jonas.

"Be careful Paw, I will start setting up camp after I water the mules," said Crockett.

Jonas gave him a nod, and answered with one word, "Good!"

Jonas rode off up the road after he had scanned around the entire area. Crockett watered the mules and brought them up close to the wagon, before hobbling them for the night. Next Crockett got out the things they would need for the night's camp. He set up the tent on a level knoll just ahead of the wagon. He then gathered some stones to put around the fire place just below the tent.

He walked around the edge of the woods gathering dry wood from the trees. Dead limbs still on a tree make the best fire wood, because it is dried out. Limbs on the ground are often wet and rotting. After getting the wood back to the fire place, he gathered a little tinder from the bark of a cedar. He ruffled it up between his hands and placed it in the center of the circled rocks.

He got out his fire starting kit. It was a file, a piece of flint, and a burned piece of flannel. He lay the burned flannel over the fluffy tinder, held the file at a forty five degree angle and struck it with the flint. A shower of sparks streaked to the burned flannel and some caught as little red dots of fire.

Crockett carefully picked up the tinder with the flannel holding the little fire. He gently blew the spark into the tinder, first there was smoke then a flame appeared. He dabbed out the sparks on his burned flannel. He put little branches on the little flame. He added fuel as the fire grew. He put his flint and steel, and burned flannel back into his water proof bag for future use.

In a little while Crockett heard a horse trotting, he looked up to see Jonas coming down the turnpike. Crockett waved his hand to acknowledge that he seen Jonas coming.

Jonas gave a quick wave, and rode Jake to the water. After he watered Jake he walked him up to the camp.

As Jonas unsaddled and hobbled Jake, Crockett smiled and asked, "See anything

Crockett's Long Trip To Kentucky

Paw?"

"Nothing to be too alarmed about," answered Jonas.

"About five miles up the road I seen where somebody scattered out some clothes and broke up some wooden boxes, exclaimed Jonas.

"What do you make of it Paw?" asked Crockett.

"Either people threw out their trash, or bandits went through their catch," replied Jonas.

"There were several tracks, horses and men's" said Jonas, "of course wagon tracks too."

"Since this is the road to Kentucky, there would be wagon tracks," said Jonas. "I don't think we should be too alarmed," Jonas added.

"How about the road, is it any better?" asked Crockett.

"Not much, if it don't rain it will get better each day," suggested Jonas.

"Did you see them fish down in the river Paw?" asked Crockett.

"Yes I did see some, bet we could catch some for breakfast, or may be even supper," answered Jonas.

"Let's cut us a pole and give it a try," replied Jonas.

"I was hoping you would say that, I gathered some worms while getting the rocks for the fire place," replied Crockett.

"Good," answered Jonas, "I think they are bronze backs, they always give a good fight and are tasty to eat."

"That means they are Small Mouth Bass, don't it Paw," said Crockett.

"Yes," answered Jonas, "that's just a nick name I reckon!"

Crockett's Long Trip To Kentucky

Jonas and Crockett cut themselves a long limber sapling and tied on a line with hook and sinker. They walked to the edge of the water cautiously not to scare the fish. They gently flipped out a wiggling hooked worm for an offering to the active fish. Almost instantly both had a flipping shaking fish on their hooks. Jonas got out a piece of cord he brought with him from the wagon. They strung up the two Bass; and sent out another offering.

In about twenty minutes they had caught six nice Small Mouth Bass.

Jonas smiled at Crockett, "looks like we will have fish for supper."

"Yes it does Paw, do you think anybody ever fished here before?" asked Crockett.

"Probable Indians, or Tice Harmon," replied Jonas.

Tice Harmon, the Frontiersman?" asked Crockett.

"Well this is his old stomping ground," replied Jonas.

"I will tell you about him after supper," said Jonas.

"We got to get these fellers fried up, it is going to get dark on us real soon," added Jonas.

After a good hot meal of fried fish, and fried corn cakes the two sat back to enjoy the moment. Jonas takes a chew from his plug. He meticulously placed it way back in the right side of his jaw. Crockett watched, but never asked for any. He was remembering the chew he tried a few days ago. Crockett was thinking how good that looked, yet it will make a fellow sick! Jonas looked at him, and smiled, as if reading his mind.

"Well now Paw, tell me about that Harmon feller," said Crockett.
"Tice Harmon is his name, he did a lot to open up this western land," Jonas said.
"I know what you are thinking when I say western land," Jonas added.

Jonas explained that this area is still more primitive than some point's way out west.

Crockett's Long Trip To Kentucky

Jonas told the story about Tice living up in the Abbs Valley section of Tazewell County back in the 1780's. Tice hated the Indians and the Indians feared and hated him.

Tice use to bring a hunting party back in here and up the Big Sandy most every fall. They could get all the meat and bear grease they needed in a short time. He had a camp set up and used it every winter.

A band of Indians were aiming to capture Tice, and burn down his place up in Abbs Valley, but they went to the Wiley cabin by mistake. They ran in on Jenny Wiley, her little brother, and about four other young-uns. They killed all of them except Jenny and the youngest baby. Jenny was expecting at the time. They grabbed up what they could easily carry and took off with Jenny. They headed across the mountains toward Tug Fork, in the direction of the Ohio towns.

Tice found out about it, and got some men together and followed them to the Tug Fork. It was swelled up with flood waters and they could not get across, so they had to give up.

The Wiley cabin never burned down, it was wet from recent rains and the Indians were in a hurry to get away before Tice found out.

To make a long story short, Tice was back over here on the Big Sandy the next year. Guess what, Jenny got lose from the heathens and ran for days through the woods and run up on the Harmon camp. Tice and his long knives, as the Indians called them, took Jenny right back to her husband. Even before that Tice set up an ambush over on Russell Fork, not far from here. They killed most of the Indians, and the rest ran off, back to the Ohio country.

I have never been there but, Tice set up a station north west of here a few miles. They call it Harmon Station. Ole Tice loved this rugged country and the bountiful supply of game. So he just moved over here.
"Is Tice still living," asked Crockett?

"Well I don't know for sure, but I would guess he has passed on, but no red skin ever got his hair," answered Jonas.

"What about Jenny Wiley, did her babies make it," asked Crockett?

Crockett's Long Trip To Kentucky

"No" answered Jonas.
Jonas explained that the Indians took the baby by the heels and bashed its brains out on a tree when they were running from Tice. The other baby was born in a Indian hunting came. The Indians tested it to see if it would be brave. The little feller cried, and it was killed also.

"Paw," asked Crockett, "how did she get away from the Indians?"
Jonas explained that they left her in camp by herself after a while. She had a dream about running off. Something about two trails in the woods, a bird flew down on a certain trail. It was like God telling her the direction to run.

She got up and after the Indians went out to do their mischief, she quietly slipped away. The story goes that she came up on the two trails at a fork. She did not know the best one to follow. As she stood there looking, a bird flew down on the left trail. She remembered the dream; the decision was made by that little bird. She ran for several days and came up on the Big Sandy River. Low and behold, there was Tice Harmon's hunting camp. Ole Tice thought she was an Indian because she wore buck skins and had a deep tan from the sun. Finally he took her under his protection and they headed for the safer country, now Tazewell County.

Crockett sat there with his big gray eyes shining. He enjoyed each and every word of the Jenny Wiley story.

"Paw is there any Indians around here anymore," asked Crockett.

"No son, they are few and far between," answered Jonas.

"Most of them are out in the western areas of this country, you remember about the trail of tears grand paw Hezekiah told you about don't you," asked Jonas.

"Was Jackson a bad president," asked Crockett?

Jonas explained that in some ways he was. A lot of folks didn't agree with him, when he rounded up all the Indians he could, and marched them to the west. One reason he done that, I heard was the discovery of gold in northern Georgia. The White men wanted the Indian lands to get the gold.

Crockett's Long Trip To Kentucky

"Paw that is awful," exclaimed Crockett.

"I guess it is," answered Jonas.

"We better get ready for bed, did you put the feed bags on the mules for a while son?" Jonas asked.

"Yes I did, I took them off right after supper," Crockett said, "the mules and Jake are just enjoying the new green grass now."

"Good," said Jonas, "now I want you to lay that shotgun close to your bed so you can get it in a hurry."

"Paw do you think some bad men will attack us tonight?" asked a serious Crockett.

"No son I doubt it, but we must be ready just in case," answered Jonas.

"Now go to sleep and have a good dream," Jonas added.

"I might dream about Jenny finding her trail with the help of that bird, that God sent her," answered Crockett.

"Good night son, and don't forget to talk to God," Jonas said.

"He deserves our thanks and praise; and ask Him to look over us while we sleep," added Jonas.

"I will Paw, and good night to you, Oh! I might dream about Virginia too," said Crockett.

Crockett's Long Trip To Kentucky

Chapter 3
Kentucky Border

Next morning Jonas woke up first. He scanned the area to make sure everything was as it should be. He put some kindling on the fire, and a piece or two of fire wood. He went up into the woods to relieve himself. He noticed that he had an audience, of squirrels, chip monks, birds and a young deer. Jonas thought to himself, how wonderful, God has made things. I would have loved to have seen the Garden of Eden!

Crockett pulls the big quilt up under his chin, and peers out at the new morning.

"You going to sleep all day," asked Jonas?

"Well Paw, it does feel good laying here in my warm bed," answered Crockett.

"Get up son, it's not too cool once you get your clothes on; I got the fire fixed up," said Jonas.

Crockett crawled out and yanked on his britches.

He looked around, and smiled, "looks to be a fine day," he exclaimed.

"Yes it does," said Jonas.

The mules and Jake were all in sight, and still grazing on the new spring grass.
    The Whitt's ate a hurried breakfast, and broke camp. In a short time they were moving down the pike towards Kentucky.

Jonas wanted to make good time today if the road would permit it. The last few days the mushy, rutty road slowed progress.

As they rode along Jonas started a conversation.

"Well did you have that dream last night?" asked Jonas.

"I don't know Paw," asked Crockett?

Crockett's Long Trip To Kentucky

"Seems like I did but can't remember it," Crockett said.

"I do that sometimes," answered Jonas," I had a dream last night."

"What was it about?" asked Crockett.

"I dreamed we were in Kentucky, up on the Big White Oak Creek, and we were there building the mill, and Indians were sulking about watching us," Jonas said. "Indians Paw, thought you said the Indians were gone," exclaimed Crockett.

"Well son it is a dream, not real," Jonas said.

"Do you want to hear it or not?" Jonas asked.

"Sorry Paw, yes I do," answered Crockett.
Jonas went on with the dream, explaining that he asked the Truitt's about the Indians. They said don't worry, they are just spirits. Spirits, I ask, what does it mean? The Truitt's said that once up on a time the Indians hunted and fished there on the farm. Now sometimes we see their spirits watching over the land.

"Was it scary?" asked Crockett.

"No it seemed peaceful," answered Jonas.

"Then I met a woman, she was young and beautiful, well I have to say she turned my head, ain't this a weird dream," asked Jonas?

"What else happened in your dream?" asked Crockett.

"I dreamed that you and me and some other folks dug a trace off the creek and built an under shot grist mill, it was working beautifully," said Jonas.

"Mister Truitt was so happy; he gave us a bonus of a piece of his land." Jonas continued.

"What does it all mean Paw?" asked Crockett.

"Probably nothing, it was just a dream," answered Jonas.

"Sometimes we just dream up a mess of stuff," Jonas said.

"There is no Indian Spirits lurking around, nor is there a young woman that would notice me," Jonas explained.

"Your Maw is the love of my life, I don't expect to settle down with another woman, especially a young one," added Jonas.

"I guess I ate too many bass," said Jonas.

Crockett laughed!

"They were fun to catch, wasn't they Paw?" asked Crockett.

"Fun to catch and good to eat," Jonas said, "the good Lord provides for his children.

The morning passed quickly, and for once they made good time. The mules had a much easier pull in this rocky stretch of road. There were still patches of soft ground, but the going was better.

They passed the debris that Jonas seen yesterday and the road improved. Jonas was really pleased to be making better time. He told Crockett that in another day they should be in Kentucky.

"That will be great Paw," exclaimed Crockett.

"How far do you think it will be to Floyd County where Uncle John lives?" asked Crockett.

"I think we can be there in less then two weeks, maybe in around a week," answered Jonas.
"It just depends on how many miles we cover each day; I still don't want to over work the mules," he replied.

Crockett's Long Trip To Kentucky

"I think this is the most distance we have traveled in one day," said Jonas.

"It is about 6:00 PM, so let's look for a night camp," Jonas said.

Crockett saw a rock house (over hanging rocks) up ahead.

"What about there?" Crockett said, as he pointed to the rock house.

"Pull up there Paw?" Crockett asked.

"Yelp, It will be alright, I reckon," replied Jonas.

"Not much grazing here but otherwise it should serve us for the night." Jonas added.

Crockett headed the wagon up on the hill close to the out crop of rock. He set the brake and they both got down while looking the area over. Jonas was looking at two things, shelter and a place for defense if it was needed. They had not seen any one coming or going since they left the James Thompson farm.

"Tomorrow I think we will be heading around Grapevine Mountain," replied Jonas.

"That is where some folks have been waylaid," Jonas said, "I don't want you to be scared, but be ready for any trouble that may come our way."

"Don't worry Paw, I am ready, if any outlaws show up, this old shotgun has become my best buddy," Crockett said.

"Well son that is good; I am going to saddle up Jake and take a little ride up the road a piece," said Jonas.

"Go ahead and start setting us up for the night," instructed Jonas.

"Oh! And be careful raking around under that rock house, Rattlers are probably waking up from the winter," Jonas cautioned.

"That is good to know Paw," replied Crockett.

Crockett's Long Trip To Kentucky

Jonas was on Jake and trotting down the road in short order. That is a great saddle horse, Crockett thought. Crockett admired Jakes beautiful gait.

Crockett got a stick about five feet long and headed to the rock house. He cautiously raked back the leaves from under the overhanging rock. He over turned anything that might be hiding a creepy crawler. After he was satisfied that there were nothing sleeping in his intended bed, he cleared out a spot for a fire in front of the rock house.

Next Crockett took care of the team. He unhitched them and took them down to the river for a drink. Then he gave them their feed bags with a nice portion of oats and some shelled corn.

Then Crockett unloaded the things that they would need for the night, always keeping the old scatter gun handy. He gathered kindling and fire wood for the camp fire. He lit the fire and put on some coffee.

It wasn't long before Jonas was riding back into camp.

Crockett seen him from a distance and recognized him instantly. He threw up his hand and Jonas answered by doing the same. Jonas took Jake to the river and let him drink. Then he led him up the hill and let him have his feed bag.

Jonas had a serious look on his face, so Crockett asked, "What is it Paw?"

"I seen another place that looks like some folks were robbed, furniture busted up, clothes scattered around," Jonas said.

"It looked like at least three sets of tracks," replied stated.

"What are you thinking Paw, "asked Crockett?

"Well I think we start taking turns staying on watch, and even in camp," commanded Jonas.

"One working and one was holding a gun," Jonas said, "it may not be necessary but I ain't taking no chances."

Crockett's Long Trip To Kentucky

"Well that will keep any outlaws from catching us off guard," answered Crockett.

"Better to be safe than sorry, you set over there with your gun, and I will fix supper," said Jonas.

"Alright Paw, I will watch closely, no one will sneak up on us," affirmed Crockett.

Jonas rustled up some supper while Crockett sat and watched in a panoramic motion. Jonas could tell that Crockett was taking him seriously about potential danger, and was proud of him. Jonas filled both tin plates and moved over to sit with Crockett and eat.

While eating, Jonas struck up a conversation with Crockett.

"Didn't find anything under the rock house that we would mind sleeping with did you?" asked Jonas.

"No Paw, I looked real close, and found nothing under there to be alarmed about," replied Crockett.

"Well son it pays to be sure about everything in this world, you are learning that aren't you," asked Jonas.

"Yes Paw, just like you say, better safe than sorry, I don't intend to let no bad men get a jump on us," Crockett said.

"Do you want me to take the first watch tonight?" Crockett asked?

"Why don't you hobble the horse and mules and stretch your legs, I have my pistol on," replied Jonas.

"Paw, I was thinking, reckon we should tie them up close to us, someone might try to steal them!" exclaimed Crockett.

Jonas leaned over and scratched his head.

"Son you have a point, stretch a line between those two trees and tie them up,"

Crockett's Long Trip To Kentucky

Jonas said.

"Crockett refill their feed bags, since they can't graze tonight," added Jonas.

Crockett smiled proudly, Paw is taking my advice, he thought. I must be growing up.

And for no apparent reason, as Crockett got up to tie the animals, his mind wondered. He thought of Virginia and her beautiful shiny black eyes. That girl sure did impress me he thought.

Jonas asked in an urgent voice, "What are you doing?"

"Are you day dreaming again?" asked Jonas.

"Well I guess I was Paw, I will get them fixed up," answered Crockett.

By now it was starting to get dark, Crockett finished up with the animals and came back to sit by Jonas. They sat and talked for about an hour about one thing then another. They talked about their trip, about being ready for trouble if it came. They talked about Greenup County and the work that lay ahead. They talked about the loved ones left behind. They even talked about Hezekiah and Rachel. Then Jonas gave Crockett his orders for the night.

"Here son, you hold on to my watch, and when it gets midnight you get me up," Jonas instructed.

"You have never let me use your watch before, I will be real careful with it, and I will wake you up at exactly midnight," Crockett responded.

"Crockett you are practically a man I can trust you with a watch or even my life," answered Jonas.

Crockett's heart swelled with pride that his paw trusted him this much. Jonas smiled as he crawled into his quilts under the rock house.

"See you at midnight son," said Jonas.

"Sleep good Paw, and I will be a good watch," said Crockett.

Crockett's Long Trip To Kentucky

Crockett kept the fire and stayed vigilant. He would get up and take little walks around the camp, but was real quiet not to wake Jonas. He thought about the adventure he was on, and wondered what lay ahead. We might get to the Kentucky border tomorrow or next day for sure, he thought. I will be glad to get away from this troublesome area, he reflected. Time went fast, and before he knew it was 12:05 midnight.

Crockett went over close to where Jonas slept.

"Paw, paw, are you ready to get up?" Crockett asked.

"What is it son, is anything wrong, is it midnight?" asked the drowsy Jonas.

"Yes Paw it is midnight, I got you some coffee on the fire," said Crockett.

"Good boy," answered Jonas.

Jonas got up and pulled on his overalls. Went out behind the wagon and took care of business. He came over and sat down by the fire and poured himself a cup of hot coffee.

"Crockett go ahead and lay down, did you notice anything out of the ordinary?" asked Jonas.

"No Paw it has been quiet except for the frogs hollering, and I heard an owl, I think," answered the sleepy boy.

Jonas laughed a little.

"Them frogs are courting, or trying to find a mate to court," Jonas exclaimed.

"They do this every year in the early spring," Jonas added.

"How long ago has it been since you heard the hoot owl?" Jonas asked.

"About two hours I would think," answered Crockett.

Crockett's Long Trip To Kentucky

"Did you just hear it once?" asked Jonas.

"It hooted two or three times, but there was no answer from another direction," Crockett said.

"I know what you are asking, I am sure it was the flying kind of owl," added Crockett.

"Alright son, get you some sleep, I will watch over you," said Jonas.

"Paw," Crockett said.

"What is it son?" asked Jonas?

"Nothing, I just wanted to tell you I love you," said the sleepy Crockett.

"I love you son, now go to sleep, I will see you first light," answered Jonas.

The night passed by quickly. There was nothing going on that seemed threatening, to the two travelers. Jonas built up the fire and got some coffee brewing. Then he went over and untied the mules and Jake so they could graze for a while. There was limited grass at this camp, but the animals were glad to be free for even a short time. Crockett heard the animals and Jonas moving around and raised up.

"Time to get up Paw?" he asked.

"Yelp," answered Jonas.

"You might as well get up and get ready to head out," said Jonas.

"With good luck we will be in Kentucky today," Jonas exclaimed.

"I am ready for that," answered Crockett.

"Did anything happen while I was asleep?" asked Crockett.

"I heard your owl, and frogs, but that was about it," Jonas answered.

Crockett's Long Trip To Kentucky

"Get any sleep son?" asked Jonas.

"Think I did pretty good, but it seems like I just laid down," answered Crockett.

The two eat a hurried breakfast, broke camp, and were once again moving toward the Kentucky border. It looked like rain may be heading in their direction. They laid out their slickers, and kept their guns ready with a greased raw hide hoods over the hammers. They had one Brown Betsy, the shot gun, and Jonas' revolver loaded and ready.

There was not much conversation it seemed they were both in a serious state of mind. Even the mules were glad to be back on the road for some reason.

"That mountain on the right has to be Grape Vine," said Jonas.

Why do they call it that Paw?" asked Crockett,

"Well I don't know for sure, but I would guess it is because the road is crooked," said Jonas.

"Could be there is a lot of wild grape vines' growing on it," added Jonas.

"Does the road travel up on the mountain?" asked Crockett.

"Mister Thompson told me about a trail across it, but we will follow the road by the river," said Jonas.

"It will be further but safer, only thing the outlaws have struck travelers on the road," said Jonas."

"Since we have a heavy wagon the best bet is down here, not on the little trail across the mountain," exclaimed Jonas.
"We will be fine just stay alert as to what is going on around you, I want you to glance behind us every now and then," said Jonas.

"I will, I will look in every direction, Paw," said Crockett.

Crockett's Long Trip To Kentucky

"Good idea, I have to watch the mules and the road," said Jonas.

They fell into the normal routine of travel with the exception of added vigilance. Jonas tried to act as normal as possible for Crockett's benefit, while still being very watchful.

Crockett turned to Jonas and said, "it will be alright Paw, we prayed this morning before we left."

"The Lord will watch over us won't He," asked Crockett?

"He sure will, but He also wants us to look out for trouble," replied Jonas.

Before they knew it the morning was gone and the miles were being covered in good time. They stopped only once so far to stretch and take care of the mules. Jonas stood watch while Crockett watered them as they crossed a creek that fed the Levisa.

Nothing out of the ordinary occurred. They kept the wheels on the wagon turning and before they knew it, they saw a shabby road sign ahead.
"Can you read it?" Jonas asked Crockett.

"Yes Paw, all it says is KENTUCKY," exclaimed Crockett.

"You would think it would say more than that," added Crockett.

As they got closer they also saw a sign on the other side of the road.

Jonas turned around as they passed the signs.

"That one says VIRGINIA, I don't know what I was expecting, but I feel disappointed!" exclaimed Crockett.

"At least they have a sign," said Jonas.

The two kept moving and being very watchful. They eat leftovers as they traveled. Jonas was anxious to get out of this area. It was almost like wilderness. They had

Crockett's Long Trip To Kentucky

not passed one wagon or even a traveler since they left the Thompson's.

Crockett kept watching round about! Something caught his eyes up ahead in the edge of the woods. The sun shown into the woods and a bright but small object sent a glimmer of warning to Crockett.

"Paw, I see something shinny up ahead in the woods, I think it might be a gun, whispered Crockett.

Jonas strained his eyes and saw the same thing.

Whoa," Jonas commanded the mules.

The mules stopped, almost in their tracks.

"Crockett get that scatter gun up and point it towards them," said Jonas.

Crockett raised the gun and held it at waist level.

Jonas brought out the 44 revolver and laid it between him and Crockett.

Jonas took a quick survey of the entire area, even behind them. Seeing nothing, he turned back toward the thing in the woods.

After a minute, which seemed much longer, Jonas hollered toward the woods!

"Whoever you are, come out and be recognized," yelled Jonas.

A man carrying a rifle rode out on a rough looking horse. He also looked rough. He had an untrimmed beard, and his hair was long and shaggy. He wore a slouch hat that had seen better days. His clothes were filthy buckskins, but the barrel on his gun was shining in the sun.

"Hello stranger," he shouted.

Jonas hollered again, "what is your business, why were you hiding in the woods?" The man rode closer and answered," I am a trapper; I have been out checking my traps."

"Hold it right there, don't come any closer," commanded Jonas.

The rider stopped and glared at Jonas and Crockett.

Jonas gave instructions in a loud voice, "You turn that horse around and get away from us."

"If we see you again we will shoot first and ask questions later," yelled Jonas.

The man glared once again, then wheeled his mount around slowly. He was in no hurry to get out of sight. Instead of heading back into the woods he went toward the river.

Jonas and Crockett sat and watched the man slowly cross the Levisa and head up into the woods on the other side.

Jonas started the mules pulling the wagon again. They moved at a slow pace, and watched vigilantly all around.

"Paw, do you think he is gone away?" asked Crockett.

"It appears that way, but beware of trouble ahead, and behind," answered Jonas.

"That jasper may cross back behind us, and he could have help waiting ahead of us," said Jonas in a low voice.

Crockett's heart was pumping very fast as adrenaline filled his being. He was looking in all directions with a renewed sense of apprehension.

As they moved down the road, Crockett asked Jonas, "Why are we going so slow?"

"Don't we want to get away from here?" asked Crockett.

"We are better off moving slowly, we don't want to panic and run into an ambush ahead," replied Jonas.

Crockett's Long Trip To Kentucky

"Plus we look like we ain't scared of anything, just sit up straight and look like you ain't afraid of anything." Jonas instructed.

Crockett straightened, and casually looked around.

"That's it," affirmed Jonas.

"By the way your keen eyes may have saved us back there, I did not see that feller up in the woods," Jones exclaimed.

"Thanks Paw, I am trying to spy anything else that may be a danger," Crockett said.

Up ahead the woods came down to the road on both sides. It looked like a likely spot to be jumped. The wagon moved even slower. Jonas and Crockett strained their eyes to see anything that may be lurking in the woods. Nothing could be seen, not even a bird.

"It is too quiet and still" said Jonas.

"What do you mean by that?" asked Crockett.
"No birds or animals mean, there could be a man is hiding there," answered Jonas.

"Raise the scatter gun a little higher, if someone is there I want them to consider, that we are ready for them," whispered Jonas.

Crockett raised the barrel of the shot gun in a menacing manner.

Jonas also turned and reached under the canvas cover on the wagon and pulled out the old Brown Betsy. He stuck it between him and Crockett. He also kept the revolver handy with the holster cover unlatched. The wagon continued to move slowly toward the area that looked to be a danger spot.

Jonas prayed in a low voice; "Lord be with us as we go through the valley of the shadow of death. Protect me and my boy from the pestilence, and the destruction that wasteth at noonday! Be our fortress and refuge, We trust you Lord that no evil befall us, Praise be the Name of Jesus" "Amen!"

Crockett's Long Trip To Kentucky

Crockett answered with, "Amen!"

As the wagon moved into the narrow place, two riders came around the bend and rode casually toward the Whitt's.

They look much better than the rider that they encountered earlier. When they got within twenty five yards, Jonas stopped them with a shout.

"Hold it right there," he said, as he held the cocked revolver toward them.

The riders stopped quickly and one of them spoke up.

"Sir, put down that gun, we mean you no harm!"

Crockett turned and looked back down the road.

"Paw," whispered Crockett, "that other jasper is back there watching, he is just sitting his horse there about two hundred yards back," whispered Crockett.

Jonas answered the rider that had spoken, "what is your business, where are you going?"

Then Jonas answered Crockett in a whisper, "keep an eye on him son, if he starts closing in on us let me know."

The riders kept their distance, while trying to figure out Jonas and Crockett. They begin to whisper.

Jonas hollered at them, "Stop whispering, who are you?"
"We are on our way home, we been out visiting our sick Maw," one man answered.

"I am Isaac Fleming and this is my brother Sean," he said.

"Where do you fellers live?" asked Jonas.

"We live across the mountain and up the Russell fork some folks call it Holly Creek,

Crockett's Long Trip To Kentucky

it feeds the Russell," said the one calling himself Isaac.

"Well then where is your sick Maw," asked Jonas.

"Down the river from here and up John's Creek," said Isaac.

"We used to live there with them, but decided we liked it over in Virginia better," he added.

"Sir I promise on the Bible, we mean you no harm," exclaimed Isaac.
"Crockett is that feller still back of us?" asked Jonas.

"Yes, but he is riding away from us now, I think he saw these other fellers and thinks they are with us," Crockett said in a whisper.
Jonas hollered again at the men he was holding at bay.

"How is your Maw doing?" Jonas asked.

"She is tolerable, but has had a bad winter," answered the one rider calling himself Isaac.

"Alright come on ahead, but slow," Jonas said, "if either one of you make a false move, you will be paid in lead."

Jonas also said in a loud voice, "Crockett shoot to kill if they mean us any harm!"

Crockett said, "I will," in his heaviest voice.

The riders came on at a slow pace, watching Jonas and Crockett's every move.

Jonas and Crockett kept them covered with the scatter gun and revolver.

When the riders got within ten yards, Jonas hollered again.

"Hold it right there, Isaac you come on and Sean you wait," he commanded.

"Alright mister," Isaac answered.

Crockett's Long Trip To Kentucky

The first rider came on by the wagon and moved on down the trail.

Then Jonas said, "Sean come on and don't try anything."

Sean nodded and rode forward.

Crockett kept Isaac covered with the shotgun and Jonas held the pistol on Sean.

Sean passed Jonas and moved on toward his brother.

Jonas hollered back at them, "You Fleming boys keep on riding and don't look back; sorry to treat you this way, but we can't take a chance."
    Isaac hollered back, "No problem, I don't blame you."

"Who are you fellers?" Isaac asked.

Jonas answered, "we are the Whitt's Jonas and Crockett, take care there is a shady looking man up ahead of you," Jonas warned.

"We seen him," said Isaac.

"You be careful too," replied Isaac as they rode down the turnpike.

"Shooo weee," exclaimed Crockett," I am glad that is over."

"Me too," said Jonas.

"You did real good son, but we ain't out of the woods yet, just keep an eye out for trouble," exclaimed Jonas.
"I will," answered Crockett.

"I wonder how far it is to Uncle John's house in Floyd," asked Crockett?

"We just barely got into Kentucky and you are wondering how far to John's house," said Jonas.

"I would say another week or so," Jonas said patiently.

Crockett's Long Trip To Kentucky

Jonas got the mules moving again and they were making good time. Crockett kept an eye out for trouble, looking in all directions, especially in the rear. He was afraid that some of the men may try to sneak up on them from the rear. That first encounter, the trapper, never was resolved. Crockett and Jonas both thought he was an outlaw.

The rest of the day was without incident! They calmed down and enjoyed the next few miles.

Jonas led in a prayer of Thanksgiving for the Lords protection. They both said amen together.

As the day wore on a chill filled the air! Crockett shivered, and dug under the wagon cover for their coats.

"Paw, ain't this about the ninth of April," Crockett said," It feels like February this evening!"

"Yes it is the ninth, the best I can recollect," said Jonas.

"There is some winter still left in the air, I think we better start looking for a good place to camp," Jonas said.

"Paw is Kentucky a colder place than Tazewell County, or is this just a late cold spell," Crockett asked?

Jonas explained that it is about the same, the elevation in parts of Kentucky is much lower than Tazewell County, so it should be a little warmer.

"But according to the feeling this evening, I have to wonder," Jonas said.

"I have seen late weather like this before, but it never lasts for any time," added Jonas.

"Good Grief," exclaimed Crockett," It is starting to snow!"

"I see it," said Jonas.

Crockett's Long Trip To Kentucky

"I see what looks like a good rock house up ahead," said Jonas.

"I am going to check it out," added Jonas.

"Who knows we may have some real weather tonight," Jonas said.

They pulled up on the hill and locked the brake on the wagon. It was a large rock house, almost a cave.

"Crockett, you go and check for "creepy crawlers" and I will start getting us some fire wood, before everything gets wet," instructed Jonas.

Crockett got himself a sturdy stick and raked the leaves around under the rock house. Then he cleared out a large area in front to make a place for a fire. Then he gathered some stones to circle the camp fire. By then Jonas came back carrying fire wood.

Crockett got his fire building stuff and lit a fire. Jonas began to unhitch the team and Jake his saddle horse. The snow began to pour.

"Can you believe this snow?" asked Crockett.

"Well I have seen a late snow like this a time or two, but it is highly unusual," Jonas answered.

"We need to get everything that we need for the night and put it in the dry," said Jonas!

"Crockett, you go ahead setting up camp, I am going to take the mules and Jake to water," Jonas said.

"I think we can tie them up over here on the left of the rock house," Jonas said, "the cliff will keep most of the snow off them!"

When Jonas led the animals back up the hill, Crockett had a good fire going. And had drug out the quilts, pots and pans and other items needed for the night.

"Good job," replied Jonas!

Crockett's Long Trip To Kentucky

Crockett looked at Jonas and the animals, and burst out laughing!

"What is so funny," asked Jonas?

"You look like a snow man! And the mules look like snow mules, and poor Jake is covered too," answered Crockett.

Jonas chuckled a little!

"I guess we do look funny," Jonas replied.

"It is a wet snow, and is really coming down, hopefully it will be gone soon," replied Jonas.

Crockett had some salt bacon frying and a pot of coffee brewing in short order. Jonas strung a line to tie the animals for the night. Then he filled their feed bags with oats and corn and put them on each animal. It was a pleasure to see them enjoy their supper.

Jonas was thinking about the day's events, and told Crockett, "I don't think anyone will try anything tonight, I think we can both get a good night's sleep.""

That will be great, Paw, I am wore plumb out," replied Crockett.

"Me too, after supper we can get into some warm quilts. But I want you to keep your shotgun handy, just the same," answered Jonas.
"Me and this pistol are getting to be pretty good sleeping buddies," said Jonas.

"I know what you mean Paw," exclaimed Crockett.

"This shotgun thinks it is another one of my arms or legs," Crockett said.

Jonas chuckled!

"We must stay prepared for trouble if it comes, so far we have done well," said Jonas.

The next morning Jonas and Crockett awoke to a winter wonderland. A big six

Crockett's Long Trip To Kentucky

inch wet snow had fallen and hung on every little branch. Jonas crawled out of his warm bed and started putting wood on the little fire. Crockett peeped out from under his pile of quilts.

"Wow look at that snow, Paw!" exclaimed Crockett!

"I know," said Jonas "isn't it beautiful?"

"It surely is," replied Crockett.

"Reckon we will get to travel today Paw?" Crockett asked.

"Well we will get a late start, if we do," Jonas replied.

About that time, Jonas saw two big squirrels fighting about fifteen yards away. They were either fighting over a nut or maybe territory. Jonas nodded to Crockett, as if to say, hears breakfast. Crockett raised the old scatter gun slowly and unloaded on the two unsuspecting squirrels.

"Good shot," said Jonas as he went over to get the provided meal.

He picked them up and waded back trying to step in the same tracks.

Jake whinnied, in protest at the commotion.

"It's alright boy," Jonas said to his beloved saddle horse.

Jake settled down, after hearing Jonas speak.

Crockett got his clothes and brogans pulled on and took the squirrels.

"I will get them skinned out in about two shakes of a dog's tail," said Crockett.

Jonas laughed, "We ain't got no dog!"

Crockett gave him a little grin and went to work on the furry critters.

Jonas got the fire ready for cooking by raking out some coals to the side. He got

Crockett's Long Trip To Kentucky

the coffee pot on and the skillet ready with some good hog lard melting.

They were really hungry and devoured every eatable piece of the meat. After a second cup of coffee, Jonas took himself a chew from his plug.

The snow was already melting as the sun climbed into the Kentucky sky.

"Looks like it will leave us soon, but I am afraid it will be sloppy the next few days," said Jonas.

"First April snow I ever saw," exclaimed Crockett!

Crockett's Long Trip To Kentucky

Chapter 4
Follow The Levisa

The wagon is rolling again, but not very fast! Jonas and Crockett are still being careful, watching for potential trouble from outlaws.

The snow is gone but the mud is still a problem.

They start passing a farm here and there, and this makes them feel much more at ease.

The weather is more like April now with some much wanted sunshine.

As they ride along Crockett asked questions as usual.

"Paw, what county are we in?" Crockett asked.

"Pike County," answered Jonas.

"Wonder how it got named?" asked Crockett?

"I heard someone say it was named after General Zebulon Pike," answered Jonas.

"Is it a big county, Paw?" Crockett asked?

"Yes it is, and mostly mountains, it is different than most of the rolling hills of central Kentucky," answered Jonas.
"Well Paw, I have not seen many places that would make a good farm," Crockett said.

"The ground is good, but not much flat land, I guess someday the timber and minerals will be a big thing for Pike County," Jonas said.

"What about a court house?" asked Crockett?

"Piketon is the county seat, so that is where it is some folks call it Pikeville," replied Jonas.

Crockett's Long Trip To Kentucky

"Will it be a big city, Paw?" Crockett asked.

"I think it may be about like Jeffersonville, but I really don't know," answered Jonas.

"Don't you ever run out of questions?" asked Jonas?

"Well Paw, if I don't ask how will I find out stuff?" answered Crockett?
"I guess that is right," replied Jonas.

"Paw, does Uncle John Bunyon live in Pike County?" Crockett asked.

"No he lives in Floyd County, not too far from Prestonsburg," Jonas said.

"When will we get there?" asked Crockett.

"I don't know," said Jonas.

"It depends on how far we go each day," Jonas added.

"Paw, look here comes a rider and he is making purty good time," Crockett said.

"I see him, hold to your gun; I don't think it is trouble this time," answered Jonas.

The rider slowed up as he approached the Whitts. The rider raised his hand as a friendly gesture.

Jonas waved back, but kept a keen eye on the traveler.

The rider was the first to speak as he stopped by the wagon.

"Have no fear, I am the post rider," he said.

"I got a load of mail to get delivered," He said."

"Where you fellers hail from?" he asked in the same breath.

Crockett's Long Trip To Kentucky

Jonas spoke up after noticing the bags marked with U.S.

"We are the Whitts from Tazewell County Virginia I am Jonas Whitt," Jonas said.

"What is your name?" asked Jonas.

"Silas, Silas Johnson, that is what they call me," he said.

"I deliver the mail from Piketon toward the Virginia line," Silas said.

"Where you fellers headed?" asked Silas the Post rider?

"We are going to stop and see my brother up close to Prestonsburg, but then we aim to go to Greenup County to do some Mill work," answered Jonas.

"Who might your brother be?" asked the Silas.
"My brother is John Bunyon Whitt, he lives out on a creek called Right Beaver," answered Jonas.

"My Lord is he a big strong feller?" asked the Post rider.

"Yes he is a big man, a Carpenter by trade," replied Jonas.

"I met him once, and have heard many stories about him," exclaimed Silas.

"What kind of stories?" asked Jonas?

"Nothing bad, but stories of his strength," Silas said," He don't take nothing off no body, I heard."

"I heard that six fellers attacked him and after the Donnybrook was over, only one man was standing, and that was Big John Bunyon Whitt," related Silas.

"I even heard about a bear getting a hold of him and John whipped the bear, don't know how true that story is, but it is fun to tell," said Silas the Post rider.

"Have you ever been over on Right Beaver Creek?" asked Jonas.

Crockett's Long Trip To Kentucky

"I been in that vicinity, but don't know the place John lives on," said Silas.

Jonas asked Silas the distance to Pikeville?

"I figure another two days pulling that wagon," replied Silas the Post rider.

"I would love to talk longer, but I got to get moving." said the Post rider.

"Well alright, we need to do the same thing," answered Jonas.

"Jonas Whitt, you and your boy have a good trip," Silas said in parting.

"Alright Silas Johnson, you be careful, and it was good meeting you," replied Jonas.

Crockett spoke up, "good meeting you Mister Johnson, my name is Crockett."

The Post Rider smiled and nodded to Crockett, and rode away.

"Well there is your answer," replied Jonas to Crockett, "about two more days to Pikeville."

"I would guess another week or so after that to Prestonsburg," Jonas said.

"One thing about it, we know people live in Kentucky now," said Jonas.
Now Jonas and Crockett could relax a little bit. As they traveled along they began passing more homesteads, and even more travelers.

Instead of camping out in to open, some nights they were welcomed to stay in folk's barns. One such time they had to leave before they could settle down. The barn was owned by a woman that had two other women living with her. When Jonas and Crockett stopped and ask if they could spend the night in their barn, they had no idea what would happen.

Jonas and Crockett unhitched the team and started to get ready for a night of rest. Next thing they knew the woman came out parading around almost naked.

"Oh my, what are you doing?" asked a be-fuzzled Jonas.

Crockett's Long Trip To Kentucky

"Can't you see I have a child here?" asked Jonas.

One of the women curtsies, and says; "I will make a man out of him!"

Another woman was rubbing herself all over Jonas!

"Get away Jezebel!" Jonas said in a loud stern voice.

"Crockett, hitch up the team, we ain't staying here," shouted Jonas.

The sinful harlots still followed them around even when the wagon was pulling out.

"Paw I ain't never seen women like that," said Crockett.

"Me neither," replied Jonas.

"Paw that one women exposed her breast to us," whispered Crockett.

"Just put it out of your mind, we will find another place to camp," said Jonas.

"The Bible says to run from such women and that is what we are doing," added Jonas.

Fortunately there was another farm about a mile down the road.

Jonas pulled the wagon in and a man came out to meet them.

"Sir would you mind if me and the boy slept in your barn tonight?" asked Jonas.

"Who are you," asked the man?

"Jonas Whitt from Tazewell County and this is my son Crockett," answered Jonas.

"We are traveling to Greenup County, and need a place to sleep," said Jonas.

"My name is Arthur Parker," the man replied and walked over and shook hands

Crockett's Long Trip To Kentucky

with the Whitt's.

"You are welcome to spend the night here in my barn, and do you need anything else?" asked Arthur.

"No sir," replied Jonas.

"I will build a little cooking fire outside your barn if that would be alright?" Jonas added.

"No, that is not alright," answered Arthur.

"My wife has a big pot of beans and some cornbread," Arthur said, "Y'all come on in and eat at the table."

"Sir we don't want to impose, but that sure sounds good," replied Jonas.

"No imposition," said Arthur.

"This is awfully nice of you Arthur," Jonas said as he sat down at the family table. "We are glad to share with folks when we have it to share," said Arthur.

"The beans are still hot and smell so good," said Jonas.

"This is my kind of meal," Crockett said.

As Jonas and Crockett enjoyed their beans, they began a conversation with the Parkers. They talked about this and that. Finally the subject of the three women up the road came up.

"They are pure trash," said Mrs. Parker.

"It is good that you didn't stop there," she said.

"Well we did stop there, but were on the run in short order," announced Jonas.

Arthur snickered.

Crockett's Long Trip To Kentucky

Mrs. Parker said," it ain't funny, it is a disgrace."

"Them Hussies have tried to lure my man over there," she added.

Arthur was more serious now!

"What did they do Jonas?" ask Arthur.

"They tried to, you know, seduce me and even the boy, we got out of there as fast as we could," replied Jonas.

"Even the mules got confused," said Crockett, "hitch, unhitch, hitch, unhitch."

"The mules were wondering if they were coming or going," Jonas added.

Arthur couldn't help but laugh!

"Well they can get a good rest in the barn with you fellers," replied Arthur.

The Whitts thanked the Parkers and were on the road early.

About 2:30 PM, the next day the Whitt's wound along the river and see Piketon.

"Paw, I think this must be Piketon," announced Crockett.

"It's the most buildings I have seen since we left Jeffersonville," added Crockett.

"Yelp I think you are right," answered Jonas.

"It sure is crammed down in between the mountains," added Jonas.

"We better watch our step, I hear it is a wild town," Jonas said.

"There are a lot of people in town today, wonder if something is going on?" asked Crockett.

"Something is sure enough going on," surmised Jonas.

Crockett's Long Trip To Kentucky

"There can't be this many folks that live in town," Crockett said.

"This might be Saturday," said Jonas.

Jonas explained that little towns like this sometimes fill up on Saturday. Folks come into town to shop, take care of business, or just come in looking for something to do.

"Paw did you notice about every man has a pistol strapped on?" asked Crockett.

"Yes I did, son, something is going on, answered Jonas.

"Drive the team up over there, we can go into the mercantile and pick up a few possibles," said Jonas.

"I am getting a little low on coffee and chew-backer, anything else we need?" asked Jonas.

"Don't know of anything Paw," Crockett answered.

"We might find out what is going on," said Jonas.

Crockett pulled off the road and got down. He walked to the front of the team and tied the mules to a hitching rail. Crockett followed Jonas into the store.

A lot of folks were standing around talking, not really shopping.

The merchant walked up to Jonas and Crockett.

"Sir may I help you?" he asked.

"Yes sir we need some coffee, and a couple plugs of chewing, and may be a few other things," Jonas answered.

"My name is Ebenezer Franklin, I run this little store," said the store keeper.

"I don't remember you all, are you traveling through," asked Ebenezer?

Crockett's Long Trip To Kentucky

"I am Jonas Whitt, this here is Crockett, we are on our way to Greenup county," said Jonas.

"By the way Ebenezer, what is going on in your fair city," asked Jonas.

"Jonas, glad to meet you and young Crockett, we have a hanging here today in about an hour," said Ebenezer.

Crockett looked at his Paw, and back at Ebenezer.

"You haven't heard, have you?" asked Ebenezer.

Jonas nodded his head and said, "No sir, who is doing it, the County?"

"Our district judge ordered it and we have a hangman from Lexington here to handle it," replied Ebenezer as he set a bag of coffee on the counter.

"How many are they hanging?" asked Jonas.

Ebenezer explained, "Will Lewis and John Lewis were convicted of rape and murder, and stealing two horses. They found Mrs. Sally Belcher alone in her cabin over on Tom's creek. They had their way with her then they robbed her, and killed her with a butcher knife. That weren't enough they stole their fine riding horses."

"Poor old Tom came home to find the mess and his missus all cut up, she was able to tell him who done it, afore she passed," Ebenezer stated.

"Tom Belcher went to a neighbor and had them to fetch the high sheriff, that all happened about a year ago, and now is the day them Lewis boys pay their due," said Ebenezer.

Ebenezer explained, that is why so many folks are here today. If you and the boy want to see it, it will be in the court yard beside the court house. They have a nice big gallows built up and benches set up for the folks to sit on.

"Jonas I got your coffee, and tobacco, what else can I get you?" asked Ebenezer.

"Do you have any fresh eggs, and good country ham?" asked Jonas.

Crockett's Long Trip To Kentucky

"Eggs are just starting to come in again, I got a dozen, they are a mite high though," said Ebenezer.

"How high are they Ebenezer?" asked Jonas?

"Well since I am going to close in a few minutes, I will let them go for fifteen cents," he said.

"That is high, but I will take them, we haven't had an egg since last fall sometime," replied Jonas.

"How much ham do you want?" asked Ebenezer.

"About two pounds I reckon," replied Jonas.

"Anything else I can get you Jonas?" he asked.
"Not that I can think of," said Jonas.

As Ebenezer got the eggs and ham he also got a piece of whore-hound candy out of a jar and handed it to Crockett.

"Thank you," Crockett said with a grin.

"Welcome son," he answered.

"I got to get these folks out of here so I can go watch the hanging, said Ebenezer.

Ebenezer turned around and spoke with a loud firm voice, "I am closing the store for now, and everybody is going to have to leave."
People shuffled around and headed for the door.

Ebenezer took care of the Whitt order and escorted them to the door, and then he turned the key and locked it.

"Jonas, it was nice serving you, will see you at the courthouse," he asked.

"We might be there, where is it any way?" asked Jonas.

Crockett's Long Trip To Kentucky

"Just follow the crowd about a block and a half down the street," he answered.

"Thanks and nice meeting you," Jonas said.

Jonas and Crockett walked toward the wagon, Crockett slurping on his candy.

"What do you think, Crockett, do you want to witness this execution?" asked Jonas.

Crockett looked a little doubtful.

"Let me warn you it will not be pleasant watching them fellers die, you will remember it for the rest of your life," added Jonas.

"Paw, do you think I can stand it?" asked Crockett.
"Well I do think you are man enough to stand it," said Jonas.

Jonas explained that it is part of our world to punish bad men, and it will be a learning experience for you.

The whole street was full of people gathering for the hanging. No wagons or even riders on horseback were moving.

Everyone was walking! The talking of so many people created a great roar.

Jonas pulled out his watch, and gave it a good look.

"It is supposed to happen in about fifteen minutes, we better get up there," said Jonas.

They started to walk down the crowded street, to find a place to view this awful, but just thing!

Finally Jonas and Crockett found a place to stand behind the seated people.

The Sheriff went up on the gallows and shouted out, "Quiet, Quiet!"

Crockett's Long Trip To Kentucky

The Sheriff said, "This is an official execution, and there will be no talking or jesters."

"In about five minutes the deputies will bring out the Lewis brothers for their execution, I better not hear a word from any of you or you will spend a night in jail," yelled the Sheriff.

Next thing, the court house door opened, and out came the Lewis brothers. Each had a law man holding them on each side.

They were followed by a minister who kept quoting scripture. In front of them the hangman led. The hangman was dressed in black and wore a tall black hat. The deputies were wearing gray uniforms, and the minister was also wearing black. They all walked slowly toward the awaiting gallows.

Tom Belcher and the rest of the kin from his and her family were seated on the front row. The Lewis brothers were paraded right in front of Tom and up the steps to the gallows. Will and John Lewis were escorted to the swing a way doors on the floor of the gallows.

Next the Hangman applied the noose first on Will, then on John. He pulled the noose tight on each of them. Their faces showed such dread, such as Crockett had never seen.

Next the Hangman asked if either one of them wanted to say anything before they were hanged?

Will was crying and praying at the same time, John said, "shut up" to his brother.

"Die like a man!" John said.

Next Will Lewis spoke again, as he looked down at the sad family, Tom Belcher, and the rest.

"Mister Belcher, I am sorry, please forgive me," Will Lewis pleaded!

Finally John Lewis spoke in a hefty voice, "Tom Belcher, Sorry for what I done!"

Crockett's Long Trip To Kentucky

The Sheriff read the sentence, and the minister prayed for the two Lewis men and for the Belcher family.

The Hangman walked up and put a sack over both of their heads, stepped back, and before anyone could expect it he pulled a lever and the two men were jolted into eternity.

A mournful sound rose from the spectators. It was nothing fun to see. At that moment the entire crowd wished they were someplace else.

Jonas looked at Crockett. He had his head bowed down praying.

Jonas spoke in a low voice, "You alright?"

"Yes Paw, I don't ever want to see anyone else killed," Crockett said!

"Let's get out of this place, we can get out of town, and get some distance before night," said Jonas.

"Good idea Paw," Crockett said," I just as soon forget what we just seen."
"I have seen it before, it is a necessary thing, and part of life," Jonas said.

"If the death sentence were abolished, I'm afraid the bad men would rule the earth," Jonas added.

"Just the same Paw, I ain't going to watch another hanging," said Crockett.

Jonas and Crockett got on the wagon and drove right through the crowd towards Prestonsburg. They got out of town about five good miles and begin to look for a place to spend the night.

"I just as soon spend the night out on the trail, don't know if we can find a farm any way," said Jonas.

"Me too, Paw, I have seen enough people for one day," answered Crockett.

That evening not much was said around the camp fire. Jonas and Crockett just did the usual things that had to be done without talking.

Crockett's Long Trip To Kentucky

Just before they turned in for the night, Jonas prayed a prayer of Thanksgiving and asked for mercy on the two Lewis men and their families. He also lifted up Tom Belcher and his family. He prayed that he and Crockett would never have to see people's lives taken again. He also prayed for traveling mercies and a good stay in the Kentucky lands.

Next morning a beautiful morning was theirs. The sun was shining and the birds were singing. The trees were a beautiful shade of green, with millions of little leaves revealing themselves to the world.

The dogwood trees decorated the hills with a warm white color. The temperature was warm with a slight breeze coming from the south.

Crockett sat up in his quilts, and said, "This is more like the Aprils I remember."

"It is one fine day son," replied Jonas.

"I hope to be at your Uncle John's day after tomorrow," added Jonas.
"Well I guess I better roll out and get moving," replied Crockett.

"Yes, let's see if we can get some miles behind us today," replied Jonas.

The camp fire was blazing by now and Jonas had some ham and fried eggs cooking. The coffee and smell of fresh eggs and ham stirred their appetites.

"That smells so good," said Crockett.

"Yes it does," replied Jonas as he turned the nice big yellow eggs.

"I am fixing you three eggs and three for me!" exclaimed Jonas.
Crockett replied, "Great, we can have the rest tomorrow morning."

"That is what I was thinking," replied Jonas.

"They were awful high but we only live once in this old world," Jonas said.

"It is the little things that make life good," Jonas added.

Crockett's Long Trip To Kentucky

The two travelers enjoyed their breakfast and broke camp. Even the mules were in a good mood it seemed. Jake was showing his feisty side as Jonas tied him to the back of the wagon.
This was the best day of travel they have had on the entire trip. Weather was good, the road was in good shape, and the Kentucky hills were showing a whole "nother side" of splendor.

They only stopped one time to water the animals and get out some trail food that could be eaten on the go. The two chewed on beef jerky and cracked parched corn as they traveled. The mules protested a little when they only had a short rest.

The road left the river for a while and headed up on the side of a big hill. It was a narrow, but good road.

As the road leveled out and followed the contour of the hill, they still made good time.

"Look up ahead, Paw, I see a cabin and out buildings," said Crockett.

"Yes son must be a little mountain farm it looks like the road goes real close to it," said Jonas.

"Paw it looks like an inn or store to me, I see another wagon sitting there," said Crockett.

"Well it is starting to get late in the day," said Jonas.

"We will stop and see what it is all about," added Jonas.

"Good idea Paw, my bottom is just about worn out!" Crockett said.

Crockett drives the team close to the building to a hitching post.

About that time a tall man with a difficult walk came out to greet them.

Jonas was the first to speak. "Hello there, mister."

Crockett's Long Trip To Kentucky

The man threw up his hand and waved.

"I am Douglas Adkins, I run this little establishment," he said.

"I am Jonas Whitt, and this here is my son Crockett," said Jonas.

"You fellers in need of a room and a meal this evening?" asked Mister Jones.

"Well, if you don't charge too much, we might just stay here tonight," answered Jonas.

"Come on in and have a look see, my partner is a good cook, and we ain't got bugs in our beds," Douglas stated.

Jonas and Douglas got the price out of the way.

"Crockett, you go ahead and start unhitching the team, I will be right out and help you", said Jonas.

Jonas went in and checked out the room, and asked what was for supper?

Douglas told him, they had some good stew, cornbread, and apple cobbler.

He stated to Jonas, "We got coffee, tea, and milk to drink; I also have some good shine, to settle you in for the night."

"You fellers put your animals in the barn, feel free to give them the hay and oats you will find out there," said Douglas.

"Have your boy draw some more water and fill up the watering trough, so they can get a drink," added Douglas.

"Thanks Mister Adkins, I will be back in shortly; we will be ready to eat before long," replied Jonas.

"Call me Doug, Mister Whitt," he said.

Crockett's Long Trip To Kentucky

"Fine," said Jonas, "you may call me Jonas."

In a short time the animals were taken care of, and the Whitt's were in the Inn.

"Smells good," said Crockett.
Doug walked over to the fire place and got the pot of stew. He brought it over and set it on the table. Next he got a half of a pone of cornbread from another counter and set it on the table.

"You fellers sit right down and eat all you want; I will fetch you some cobbler and something to drink," said Doug.

After Jonas prayed and asked a blessing on the food, and for this house; they dug into the hot meal.

"This is a fine supper!" Jonas remarked.

Doug replied, "Thank you."

"My partner is a fine cook, she is not here right now," said Doug.

"Went to see her folks for a little spell", Doug added.

Doug explained that she just left today, and she will be sorry that she missed you fellers.

After supper Jonas took a chew and moved over by the fire place where spitting would be handy.

Crockett was still working on the tasty cobbler.

Doug got down his little brown jug and set it on a little table beside Jonas.

"Mind if I join you Jonas?" Doug asked.

"Come on and join me, we might open up a keg of something," replied Jonas.

"Keg?" asked Doug?

Crockett's Long Trip To Kentucky

"Conversation," replied Jonas.

"Oh! I see said the blind man," replied Doug.

Jonas chuckled!
Jonas told Doug about the trip they were on, and where they had traveled from.

"Tazewell County, that is where I was born, but it was Russell or maybe Montgomery back then," said Doug.

"This world is getting smaller every day," added Doug.
    Crockett was listening, and wondered what that meant? How can the world get small, he thought?
Jonas told Doug about John Bunyon Whitt living up on Right Beaver Creek.

"Is he a big strong feller?" asked Doug.

"Yes he is a big man," replied Jonas.

"I have heard of him, he is well known in these parts," said Doug.

"Good man I hear, and he don't take nothing off nobody," Doug added.

"Sounds like him," said Jonas.

"I know where that is, I figure it is about ten to twelve miles from here, you all should be able to make it there tomorrow," said Doug.

"Sounds good," replied Jonas, as he spit a well-aimed ambeer in the fire.

"Now Douglas," how did you wind up here? "Asked Jonas?

Doug explained how he got this land.

"I have been here for some time now," Doug said," I came here with my Paw back about 1814."

Crockett's Long Trip To Kentucky

"I was too young to fight in the war of 1812, but Paw did," Doug said.

Doug explained that his Paw came here on the way to join the militia.

"He got this whole mountain for his service, so we settled here, said Doug. "When he came here the Indians were still sulking around trying to burn out the settlers.

"I don't remember too much about it, except the for stories my Paw told!," Doug added.

Crockett spoke up, "My Grand paw Hezekiah Whitt was an Indian fighter in the War of Independence."

"He also helped start Tazewell County as a Justice, and he is a famous man around Tazewell County," Crockett said boastfully.

"I have heard of your Grand Paw. He is a famous man, is he still living," asked Doug?

"No sir, Grand Paw went to glory last March, I mean 1846," explained Crockett.

"Sorry to hear it, he must have lived a long life," answered Doug.

Jonas interrupted, "eighty-six, and a long good life".

After the three talked about this and that, Jonas said, *"to bed, to bed, said sleepy head, oh no said slow, put on the pot said greedy gut and we will eat before we go!"*
Doug had a good laugh, after hearing this little saying.

"Does that mean you want to eat again, Jonas," he asked?

"Oh no! Just a little Whitt saying, huh Crockett?" said Jonas.

Crockett had a big smile on his face.

Early next morning, Jonas and Crockett were awakened to the aroma of bacon

Crockett's Long Trip To Kentucky

frying, and coffee cooking!

After a good breakfast the two travelers were ready to get going.

Jonas asked the Inn keeper to give him the directions to Right Beaver Creek, and to the home of his brother John Bunyon Whitt.

"Well it is purty simple, go on down the Levisa towards Prestonsburg, about five miles or so from here you will see where Beaver Creek runs into the Levisa," Doug said.

"Old Bill Adkins will be there about with his ferry boat," Doug continued.

"Just holler fer him and he will take you across, you got to cross the Levisa some place any how to get to Greenup County," Doug said.

"Tell old Bill where you are headed so he will put you out on the right side of Beaver," Doug instructed.

"There be a road on both sides of Beaver Creek," said Doug.

"Head up Beaver fer about four miles and the creek splits, you take the right one, that be Right Beaver," Doug continued.
"Your brother John Bunyon Whitt lives up the creek a couple of miles at a place called Maytown," Doug continued.

"It is a nice level valley right smack in the hills," Doug said.

"Do you understand Jonas?" asked Doug.

"I think we can find it, thanks for everything," replied Jonas.

Jonas and Crockett were on the move again and it was another nice spring day.

The morning was passing fast.

They rambled around the hillside road and back down into the little valley beside the river. They enjoyed the spring weather and the smell in the air.

Crockett's Long Trip To Kentucky

"Look up ahead Paw, I think I see the ferry boat," Crockett announced..

"I see it too," replied Jonas.

"It looks like Mister Adkins is waiting for us," said Crockett.

As Jonas and Crockett rode up, the figure of a tall bent man stood up and waved a welcome.

Jonas and Crockett both waved back.

As they got within speaking distance the man spoke to the Whitt's.

"Good morning fellers," said Mister Adkins.

"Morning to you," replied Jonas.

"We are the Whitt's, you must be Mister Bill Adkins," said Jonas.

"Yelp," said Bill.

"You fellers needing to cross the river?" Bill asked?

"Yes Mister Adkins, we are heading up Beaver and on up Right Beaver," answered Jonas.

"Well I need to put you off on the right side of the creek, that will take you to Right Beaver, just follow the road up the creek," Bill said.

Jonas carefully drove the team right on the ferry. He had to untie Jake and move him up beside the wagon.
Bill Adkins closed the gate on the back of the barge like boat. Then he took the rope and begins to pull it toward the back. The boat slowly begins to move.

"Do you want us to help you pull on the rope?" Jonas asked.

"Most folks like to help me get them across," replied Bill.

Crockett's Long Trip To Kentucky

The mules began to protest, they had never left dry land before.

Jonas helped Bill pull the rope, and he had Crockett go to the front and hold the mules. Crockett talked to them in a soothing voice. The mules calmed down and took the ride as if they enjoyed it. Jake acted up a little, but settled down as he saw the mules get quiet.

When they reached the landing, Bill went to the front and dropped the gate. Crockett led the team out on dry land. Their eyes were still wide, and their nostrils flared, but were no worse for the ride. They seemed to know that their feet were on solid footing, and felt relieved.

Jonas laughed with a little nervous excitement after they were safe on the other side.

"I thought we were all going swimming there for a while," Jonas said.

"Critters act up a might sometimes," Bill replied.

"I guess my mules have never rode a boat before," replied Jonas.

"I had a horse jump through the front gate one time," Bill exclaimed.

"What did you do," asked Crockett?

"He swam, and we followed," answered Bill with a chuckle.

They all had a little laugh.

Bill gave Jonas the final directions to Right Beaver Creek, and even to the home of John Bunyon Whitt.

Jonas thanked Bill, and the travelers were on their way.

The road up Beaver Creek was not as wide or as well maintained as was the Turnpike. Jonas drove the team for now. He told Crockett to rest while he drove for a while. Crockett knew his Paw would be the better driver in this little bumpy

Crockett's Long Trip To Kentucky

trace.

It seemed to be no time at all they were coming up on the farm of John Bunyon Whitt.

Jonas and Crockett were welcomed with open arms by John, Sarah, and all the family.
Douglas was about the age of Crockett so they enjoyed the visit.
Jonas and Crockett stayed two nights, resting and allowing the animals to rest and graze on the new blue grass on John's farm. They talked about the folks back home in Tazewell County. They talked about current events, and about Kentucky.

John explained to Jonas the best way to get to Greenup County. Simply put by John was follow the Levisa. He told him about a place called Louisa not too many miles downriver. He told Jonas about the Tug Fork joining the Levisa to form the Big Sandy River. He also told him to follow the Big Sandy all the way to the Ohio River.

There is a little town at the mouth he understood with a funny name like "Catlettsburg" or something like that.

He also directed them to head down the Ohio, through another little burg called "Poage's Landing." (Now Ashland)

He also predicted with good traveling days, they should make it to the Ohio River, in less than two weeks. He figured three or four days to the town Greenup.

Jonas and Crockett got some needed rest and so did the animals.

They also got to have a good visit with blood family.

The Whitts had a really good visit, but were anxious to get started towards their goal of reaching the "Truitt Farm on Big White Oak Creek," in Greenup County.

John gave direction to get back to the Levisa without back tracking. He explained that the road was not good and you have to cross a couple of good sized hills.

One Hill was called "Hippo." He explained that the name came from people being

Crockett's Long Trip To Kentucky

afraid to cross it.

Some feller named it that because he said, "that hill has me Hippoed"

Jonas asked if it was that bad and was it safe for them to cross.

"It is not that bad, folks cross it most every day," replied John Bunyon.

Jonas and Crockett got the wagon ready and the team hitched up.
Next Jonas and Crockett went to each one of John's family giving hugs and goodbyes. It had been a good visit and both families enjoyed it.

As Jonas and Crockett got up on the wagon, Sarah came and handed them a basket of food for the journey. They were real pleased and thanked her profusely.

Once again the Whitt Pilgrims were on the move. They were headed over the trace toward "Hippo."

Crockett started the trip driving the team.

"Paw when we get ready to pass through Hippo, I want you to drive," he said.

"When we get there I will, but I bet you could do it," Jonas replied.

Jonas wanted to encourage Crockett, but felt it might be better if he took over at certain dangerous places. "Hippo" sounded like such a place.

The two pilgrims traveled up and over around and through "Hippo" without one problem. Jonas and Crockett were quite relieved with "Hippo" behind them.

They were now watching for the Levisa once again. The route they took would come out down river of Prestonsburg. Jonas and Crockett were both sorry to miss seeing the county seat of Floyd County.

Jonas and Crockett could relax a little now. The road was better, and they would be back on the main road before long. Jonas would stay vigilant, because you can never be too careful.

Crockett's Long Trip To Kentucky

Crockett started talking about their visit with John Bunyon Whitt and his family.

"Uncle John has a big carpentry shop don't he Paw?" asked Crockett.

"He sure does, and he has a lot of customers too," replied Jonas.

"He even builds fine furniture," Jonas added.

"His stuff looks great don't it Paw?" Crockett asked.

"Yes it sure does, especially that sideboard and china cabinet," Jonas explained.

"I really loved meeting Douglas," Crockett said.

"You fellers really hit it off," Jonas said.

Crockett changed the subject by asking about the stories told on John Bunyon Whitt.
"Uncle John is well known around these parts, some of the fights must have happened," Crockett committed.

"I remember him as a boy, he could lick just about any jasper in school," Jonas commented.

"He is only about three years older than me, but he has always been much bigger and stronger," Jonas said.

"I remember one time, we had a bully at school, the bully was Billy Whay, and he picked on all the younger boys," Jonas said.
"What happened, did Billy jump on you or John?" asked Crockett?

"Billy was two years older, and a little bigger than John Bunyon," Jonas went on.

"Billy made a big mistake and threw a mud ball and hit John in the center of the back," Jonas continued.

"What did Uncle John do?" Crockett interrupted.

Crockett's Long Trip To Kentucky

"He walked up to Billy and hit him square in the nose, blood spurted out and down his shirt," Jonas said.

"Did the school marm get after Uncle John?" Crockett asked.

"He didn't say a thing, because he was a little afraid of Billy too, and was glad to see him get his up-comings," Jonas answered.

"What did Billy Whay say or do after that, Paw?" Crockett asked.

"Well he didn't bother any of the Whitts after that," Jonas said.
"Did Grand Paw Hezekiah give him a whipping Paw?" Crockett asked.

"No, Paw never found out for several years, then he just laughed about it," Jonas answered.

"Grand paw never had much sympathy for a bully," Jonas added.

As they crossed another ridge late in the day Jonas saw the Levisa Fork meandering through the little valley below. It was a beautiful site with the late glimmering sunlight dancing on the water.

Jonas stopped the team and the two just sit there for about five minutes taking in the site.

"Only God Almighty could paint a picture like that son," Jonas said.
"It sure is purty, Paw," Crockett answered.

"Well let's get on down close to the river and find us a good camp for the night," Jonas suggested.

It took about another hour to descend the hill and find a suitable camp site.
"Paw, the Levisa is getting bigger down here," Crockett said.

"Yes it is, just wait till we get to Louisa, it will really grow with the Tug Fork pouring in," Jonas answered.

They set up camp just off the road under a grove of trees. The area had some

Crockett's Long Trip To Kentucky

grass for the mules and Jake to dine on.

There was no farms close by, and it seemed they were out in the wilderness, even though they knew people were not too far away. There was no rock house to camp under, so they set up the tent.

Crockett decided to take his poll and try out the fishing. He flipped over some rocks and gathered a few worms, and went down and sat on the bank. The river was a nice color for fishing, not too muddy or too clear. Crockett put on a little stick for a float and tossed it over by a submerged log. Bam, the float took off and down deep, stretching out his fishing line. Crockett set the hook and yanked out a really large crappy. Crockett yelled at his Paw to come and join him.

Jonas came over to the river bank and looked down at the busy Crockett.

"Paw this thing hit as soon as the worm dropped to him, what kind of fish is this?" Crockett asked.

"That is a crappy, and a big one at that," Jonas replied.

"We used to catch them in the New River back in Montgomery County," Jonas replied.

Crockett threw in his line and another one hit, just like before.

"I am going to get my pole," Jonas said as he turned toward the wagon.

In a short time they had a string of six to eight nice big crappies.

"Well son, looks like we will have fish for supper," Jonas announced.

"I bet we could catch a tub full the way they are biting," Crockett said.

"You know the code of fishing and hunting son," replied Jonas.

"What, You catch you clean?" asked Crockett.

"Yes, and also you don't catch more than you need," replied Jonas.

Crockett's Long Trip To Kentucky

"Yes sir, I do remember that, even though they are fun to catch," replied Crockett.

They started a fire and enjoyed the good treats from the Levisa Fork.

"Paw them crappie sure are tasty, and fun to catch, why ain't they any in the Clinch?" Crockett asked.

"Well I don't rightly know, except that this water runs into the Ohio, maybe they swim up the river," Jonas explained.

That seemed to satisfy the boy who had so many questions.

Crappy

Musky

Chapter 5
Heading For The Ohio

Morning came and the two Whitt's were on the road early. Both got a good night's sleep, and were ready to travel. The weather was taking a turn for the worse. Temperature had dropped during the night and the wind was whipping the trees.
"Must be Dogwood Winter coming on," Jonas said.

"I just hope we don't get blowed away," answered Crockett.

Even the mules laid back their ears, and protested somewhat, but kept to the task of pulling the heavy wagon.

The sky grew dark, and a hard rain hit them for about five minutes.

"This time of year, the weather just don't know what to do, so it does everything," Jonas said.

"Well Paw, it is less than a week until May, I am ready for spring to come and stay, ain't you Paw?" Crockett asked.

"Yes son I am, it is just about here," answered Jonas.

That day they had winter, spring, and fall, it seemed. The rain showers came and went, and the wind finally lay down by the middle afternoon. Now the sun was shining brightly.

"I see what you mean Paw, about the weather not knowing what to do, it has done just about everything today," Crockett said.

"Yelp, nothing surprises me about April weather," Jonas agreed.

Jonas and Crockett covered several miles this day regardless of the weather.

They came up on a farm that bordered the road. Jonas noticed that they had a nice barn and it may be a good place to spend the night.

Crockett's Long Trip To Kentucky

"Pull up here to the gate and I will ask if we can spend the night here," Jonas said to Crockett.

Crockett pulled up as instructed, and set the brake on the wagon. Just as Jonas was stepping down, a man with a shotgun stepped out the door of the house.

"Hold it right there, just get back on that wagon and head on down the road," the man commanded.
Jonas was taken aback, with the way he was treated. Jonas stepped back up on the wagon and waved his hand.

"Hello Sir, we are the Whitts traveling to Greenup County, don't mean you any harm," Jonas hollered.

The man shook the shotgun and waved it toward them.

"I don't care who you are, get your asses on down the road, I ain't got nothing fer you," he screamed.

"Let's go son, that feller is plumb crazy," Jonas whispered to Crockett.

It was not late yet so they traveled for two to three more miles and came up on another farm.

"Well son let's see if these people have any sense," Jonas said.

They pulled the wagon up to this gate, and Jonas stepped down. He opened the gate and walked toward the door. A man opened the door and stepped out, and the Whitt's saw no gun.

"Can I help you fellers," he asked in a loud voice?

"We are the Whitts heading to Greenup County, I was wondering if you might let us sleep in your barn?" Jonas asked.

"Well I guess you could," answered the man.

Crockett's Long Trip To Kentucky

"My name is Dan McCoy, open that big gate and pull your wagon on in," he said.

Jonas opened the gate and Crockett drove on in. By now Dan McCoy had walked up to Jonas and shook his hand.

"Jonas is my name, this here is my boy David Crockett," Jonas said.

"David Crockett is one fine name son," Dan said as he shook Crockett's hand.

Dan showed Jonas into the barn, and gave him corn for the animals. He showed them a meadow with a branch running through it, to turn out the team and Jake into.

"Jonas you and young David Crockett tend your animals, then come in the house, Bertha has a big pot of soup, and some corn bread cooked up, yaw are welcome to et with us," Dan announced.

"Thank you most kindly, Dan," Jonas said.
"We will take you up on it," he added.

After a bit, Jonas and Crockett had everything under control with the wagon and animals. They came to the door and knocked. A large fleshy woman opened the door.

"Clean yer feet and com on in, I am Bertha," she said.

As they came in Jonas stuck out his hand as he shuffled his feet on the rug. Crockett did the same.
"Hello Miss Bertha, I am Jonas Whitt, this is my boy David Crockett," Jonas said.

"We ain't too formal round here, jes make yer self to home," she said.

Dan was already seated at the head of the table, and motioned for the Whitts to come on over.

Bertha served up the hot soup and corn bread, and sat down by Dan.

"We don't know much about praying, would you like to offer grace Mister Whitt?"

Crockett's Long Trip To Kentucky

Dan asked.

Jonas nodded his head, and offered up a prayer of Thanksgiving.

"Thanks Jonas," replied Dan.

"Thank you Dan and Miss Bertha for your fine hospitality," replied Jonas.

After supper, the subject of the farm back up the road came up.

"That is old Bill Pruitt, he doesn't get along with nobody," Dan said.

"He won't even let his woman off the place," replied Bertha.

"The Pruitt's and the Browns back of him, have been feuding for about two years, you are lucky he didn't shoot at you," Dan explained.
The Whitts and McCoys had a long conversation about Tazewell County, Floyd County and even Greenup County. They talked about family, current events, and the unrest between the North and South.

"I hope it never comes to war, but something will happen afore long," said Dan.

"We all need to live and let live," Jonas said.

Dan had a newspaper someone had given him. There was an article about Mormons settling way out in the wilderness next to a salt lake. The article called the place Utah.
Dan wanted to show off his reading ability, so he read it to them. Jonas told him about hearing about the Mormons and some of their beliefs.

"I hear that they have as many wives as they want," added Jonas.

"More than one wife," Bertha interrupted.

"Ain't no wonder folks run um off," she added.

Dan and Jonas smiled at her reaction!

Crockett's Long Trip To Kentucky

Next morning Bertha sent Dan out to get the Whitt's for breakfast.

Bertha had a pot of oats and a pot of coffee ready. After breakfast the two men talked about the road and direction to Paintsville and Louisa.
Jonas and Crockett hitched up the wagon and got ready for the road.

Jonas and Crockett came to the McCoy's and thanked them profusely.

"Yer welcome and glad you stopped," Dan said.

"Would you offer up another prayer afore you all head out?" Dan asked.

Jonas looked a little surprised, but nodded that he would. The four of them joined hands, and Jonas prayed a Prayer of Thanksgiving and a prayer of blessing and protection on the McCoy house.

"Amen," was said by all four.

Jonas took a minute and explained to Dan and Bertha that they could pray also. He explained that God was always around and would listen to all his children.

Jonas and Crockett were on the move once again. In another day they would be getting into the new county of Johnson. It was established in 1843 and the County Seat was in the berg of Paintsville. The county was named for Richard Johnson, known as the (Father of the American Cavalry." Johnson was in politics after the war of 1812, and served in various roles.

The name of Paintsville derived from the old Paint Creek Station. There was a station set at the mouth of Paint Creek, where it enters the Levisa Fork. It is thought the area was named this, because of Indian drawings painted on the trees.

Tice Harmon from the area of East Mountain (now Bland County Virginia,) had a station in the area in the late eighteenth century. The famous Jenny Wiley was recovered from the Indians at this station.

Jonas made note that the terrain was changing to rolling hills, and larger distance between the hills. Also the Levisa Valley has swelled out to be quite wide in some

Crockett's Long Trip To Kentucky

areas.

As Jonas and Crockett rolled into Paintsville the two were anxious to see this new place on their trek.

Jonas was looking for an Inn and a place to get a good meal. Crockett was the first to see the Inn.

"Paw over there by the Trading Post, see the sign Sayers Tavern and Inn?" Crockett said.

"Yes I do, head the team over there to the nearest hitching post," answered Jonas.

Tom Sayers was the owner of the establishment, and very friendly. He was helpful by taking Jonas to the nearby livery stable. He also provided Jonas and Crockett with a room and a good meal.

After supper Jonas and Crockett had some good conversations with the locals. Jonas had a couple of drinks of store bought whiskey, and smoked a cigar. Crockett just sat back and listened to the men talk.

Things were going pretty good until a man came in and walked up to Jonas.

"Are you the one traveling through, Mister?" he asked.

"I am Jonas Whitt, and yes I am traveling toward Greenup County, what is your business?" Jonas asked.

"Folks call me Whiskey John, but my given name is John Brull," he answered.

"I was wondering if you might need you a belly warmer fer the night?" he asked.

Jonas grew angry at the proposition!

"No sir Mister Brull, I am a Godly man and I do not indulge in such goings on," Jonas said sternly.

Mister Sayers came over and politely invited Whiskey John to vacate the premises.

Crockett's Long Trip To Kentucky

"John I told you not to be coming in here and bothering my customers," Tom told him in no uncertain terms.
After Whiskey John left, Tom apologized profusely to Jonas and Crockett.

"Crockett popped up, "Paw, my belly ain't cold, but what would be bad about having a belly warmer?" he asked.

The men at the table roared with laughter.

"I guess it is about time for me and young Crockett to go to bed," Jonas said.

The men all bid the Whitt's a good night's sleep and a good journey on to Greenup County. Jonas and Crockett thanked the men and Mister Sayers, and headed up stairs to their room.

Morning came quickly, and the Whitt's had breakfast, and were ready to travel once again. The animals had a good restful night and plenty of oats and corn.

Jonas settled up with Tom Sayers and the stable man, and they were on the road once again.

"Paw what is the next town we are heading for?" Crockett asked.

"That will be Louisa," Jonas answered.

"I guess about three days, before you ask," Jonas continued.

"Paw you can read my mind," Crockett said.

"Well maybe," Jonas replied.
The weather was getting nice, almost hot in the afternoon. It was almost May 1847, and the two travelers should not get too cold on the rest of their journey.

As they rode along, Crockett talked about Kentucky and the trip thus far.

"Paw did you hear that feller back in Paintsville talking about how it got its name," Crockett asked?

Crockett's Long Trip To Kentucky

"Yes, and I thought it was interesting about the Indian paintings, didn't you son?" Jonas asked.

"Sure did Paw, what is a belly warmer Paw?" Crockett blurted out.

Jonas turned a little pink.

"Well son, do you remember back in Pike county, them three women were trying to get us to stay with them?" Jonas asked.

"Yelp, Paw, them women who didn't hardly have clothes on," answered Crockett.

"Well son, Whiskey John sells women like that for a night at a time, do you understand son?" Jonas asked.
"Is it like what married people do paw?" Crockett asked.

"Sort of son, only it is without the Lords blessing," Jonas explained.

"Remember back in Pike I told you the Bible says in Proverbs to run from Harlots?" Jonas asked.

"I understand now, I think," Crockett said.

"Them fellers at Paintsville laughed at me cause I didn't know what a belly warmer was, didn't they Paw?" Crockett asked.

"They did not know how innocent you are, and that is nothing to be ashamed of son," Jonas explained.

In the evening of the third day from Paintsville, Jonas and Crockett were coming up on Louisa.

"Paw, ain't this Louisa where the Tug and the Levisa run together?" Crockett asked.

"Yes son and I think I heard that there is a falls in the river, the name of the river from here to the Ohio is called the Big Sandy," Jonas exclaimed.

Crockett's Long Trip To Kentucky

"Is this a new county too, like Johnson County?" Crockett asked.

"It is not as new as that, I don't think," Jonas replied.

"Maybe we will learn something about it, I think at the far side we hit the edge of Greenup," Jonas added.

"You mean we are just about there?" asked Crockett.

"No son, I think it will take about another week or more to get to Big White Oak Creek," replied Jonas.

Jonas and Crockett were ready to sleep in a bed and eat a good meal by the time they got to Louisa. They found a nice Inn in Louisa. Jonas secured a room and found good care for the mules and Jake.

After a good supper, Jonas and Crockett went over to talk to some of the local men and maybe Jonas would have some spirits. Jonas led the way over and introduced himself and Crockett.

"Hello Jonas and Master Crockett," replied one of the three.

"I am Richard Alley, the gentleman to my left is Tom Pinion, and the gentleman to my right is William Bailey," Richard continued.

Jonas and Crockett both nodded hello to each gentleman.

Jonas spoke to each and called them by name.

"Are you all just passing through Jonas, or are you settling down in our fair county?" ask Richard Alley.

"We are heading to Greenup County," Jonas said.

"Well sit down and join us for some conservation," William Bailey said.

"Please do Jonas and Master Crockett," added Tom Pinion.

Crockett's Long Trip To Kentucky

Jonas and Crockett joined the three gentlemen, and Jonas had a drink with them.

After talking about work and this and that, the subject came to Lawrence County. The three men loved talking about their home county and told everything they could about it. They explained that the county was established in 1822. It was made up from Floyd and Greenup Counties.

"How did it get the name of Lawrence?" Jonas asked.

"Captain James Lawrence was a captain on a ship in the war of 1812; in a fierce battle Captain Lawrence was wounded, but he demanded that they fight on," William said.

"On June 1, 1813, Captain Lawrence coined a praise (Don't give up the ship)," Tom Pinion added.

"That is real interesting, tell us about the area," Jonas said.

"Well we are a town of three rivers you know," Richard announced.

"Yes we have heard that, two of them rivers start out over in Tazewell County Virginia," Jonas announced.

"They are little creeks over there in Tazewell County," Crockett interjected.

"I hear tell that we are bordered with Virginia, once we got here in Louisa," Jonas said.
"That is absolutely right," William Bailey agreed.

"The Old Dominion is a big old Commonwealth, ain't it gentleman?" Jonas asked.

"Yes it is and so is Kentucky, why it goes plumb to the Mississippi River," Richard said.

"How far is it to the Ohio River?" asked Jonas.

"Pulling a wagon like you got, I figure about three or four days," Richard

Crockett's Long Trip To Kentucky

answered.

"In about a day and a half you will be in Greenup County, (Boyd Now) Jonas," said Tom.

"Where you headed to in Greenup?" asked Richard.

"We are headed to Big White Oak Creek to a place called Truittville, not too far from the town of Greenup," Jonas said.

Being tired and the drink of whiskey made Jonas ready for bed. Crockett was getting a little heavy eyed also.

Jonas stood up slowly, and shook hands with each of the men.

"You must excuse us gentleman, we need to get our rest, it has been great to meet all of you," Jonas said.

Crockett did likewise, shaking each hand and nodding good night.

"Master Crockett, it was nice meeting you, you take care of your Paw, hear," Richard said to him.

"Yes sir I will," Crockett answered.

Jonas and Crockett were soon in bed and fast asleep.

Next morning before they hit the trail, Jonas and Crockett walked down to see the confluence of the Tug, and Levisa, and the one big river they produced. Jonas explained that from here to the Ohio, the river was called Big Sandy.

"Look over there across the river," Jonas said.

"What is it Paw?" Crockett asked.

"That land over there is good old Virginia," Jonas replied.
"That is amazing Paw, Virginia being way off up here!" Crockett exclaimed.

Crockett's Long Trip To Kentucky

"I wonder how my sweet heart Virginia is doing." Crockett added.

Jonas smiled.

"We better get on the road son," Jonas said.

The evening of the fourth day from Louisa, Jonas and Crockett are coming to the mouth of Big Sandy. This place is the confluence of the Big Sandy and the Ohio Rivers. Just across the Ohio River is the State of Ohio. To the east and across the Big Sandy River is Virginia.

The berg is called Big Sandy Landing, and some folks call it Catlettsburg. The south part is sometimes called Hampton city, even though there is no city there. Catlettsburg was named for the two brothers from Virginia that settled there in the late seventeen hundreds. About 1798 Alexander and Horatio Catlett came and settled here. The Post Office was opened in Catlettsburg in 1810.

"OH my goodness Paw, look how big the Ohio River is!" Crockett exclaimed.

"It is even bigger than I thought it would be," answered Jonas.

"Look Crockett, coming down the river, it's a big steam boat!" Jonas exclaimed.

"I see it Paw, look how big it is, and look at them smoke stacks putting out the smoke," Crockett said.

"Son look at the bright colors that thing is painted," Jonas continued.

As the two Whitts stood there gazing at the site, they began to hear banjo and fiddle music coming across the water. As the great boat came closer, they could see folks dancing and moving about. Jonas and Crockett had never laid their eyes on such a sight.

"Paw look at the back of the boat, it looks like a great mill wheel pushing it on the water," Crockett exclaimed.

"It is about the same, only a mill wheel is moved by water, and steam moves the wheel on the boat," Jonas explained.

Crockett's Long Trip To Kentucky

The Whitts stood there until the river boat was well out of sight down the river.

The two travelers found the Catlett Inn, and got a room for the night.

The Big Sandy Landing showed signs of much activity. The people roundabout were beginning to send and receive goods from, New Orleans and Pittsburgh.

Some of the latest folks coming down the river were the Irish. The potato famine was sending many poor Irishman to the new world. A flat boat loaded with Irish families had stopped off to spend the night, and set up a little camp of tents and lean-to's in a level area just off the landing. They were talking loudly as they gathered fire wood and began to fix their supper.
"Paw what kind of talk is that?" Crockett asked.

"Those folks are the Irish we been reading about in the papers, they are speaking English, but with an Irish accent," Jonas answered.

After supper Jonas and Crockett were sitting around talking to folks in the Tavern. A few of the Irishmen came in for a drink of spirits to sooth their nerves and give them some glee.

Crockett enjoyed listening to the Irish talk. He thought they really talked funny. As the Irish begin to talk to the American born folks, they thought the locals talked really funny.

Jonas was a little worried about his tools and equipment on the wagon even though it was rolled into the stable for the night. He was afraid the poor Irish might help themselves to something during the night.

Jonas talked to Alexander Catlett about his fears.

"Don't worry about it, the Irish are poor, but I have not heard of them taking one single thing since they have been coming down the river," Alexander explained.

"Alright Sir, if you trust them, I guess I will not worry either," Jonas said.

Jonas talked to the locals about Greenup County, and his destination. To his surprise, most of them had heard of the prosperous Doctor Samuel Truitt. They explained that it would take about five days to get to Truittville pulling a heavy wagon. They gave directions to Greenup, and from there to Truittville.

Portsmouth Ohio as seen from South Shore Kentucky in the 1850's.

Crockett's Long Trip To Kentucky

Chapter 6
Let's Go Build A Mill!

Jonas and Crockett head down the river toward the fair city of Greenup. The next little burg is not but a few miles downriver. It is called Poage's Landing. The Poage family came to the area and settled just downstream from Catlettsburg in the late seventeen hundreds. This location is now present day Ashland, Kentucky.

Something Jonas and Crockett may have seen was the Iron Furnace's and traffic to and from them. One such furnace was the Oakland. It was started by the Kouns brothers, Jacob and John in 1834. It ran until 1849.

Many furnaces were built on both sides of the Ohio River during this time. Iron ore was in the hills of Greenup County, and across the river in Ohio. The Great furnace's produced "Pig Iron" and was shipped to other areas to fabricate such things as steam engines and rail roads.

Crockett was alive with excitement. This new land along the Ohio River was like something in a story book.

"Paw someday I am going to swim this big ole river," Crockett announced.

"Let's hope you don't tempt fate like that son," Jonas replied.

"Swimming a big river like that can be very dangerous," Jonas added.

"Well Paw, if I ever do I will have somebody in a boat go with me," Crockett said.

Poage's Landing was not as big or busy as Catlettsburg. Yet there were stacks of Pig

Pig Iron ingots waiting to go out on the next steam boat. Also some black fellers were working, in a field nearby. Jonas heard from someone that they would be on hand to load and unload the boats.

Jonas and Crockett did not tarry in Poage's Landing. Late in the evening they had traveled to the John McConnell School. (Present day Wurtland, Ky.) It was a really big plantation type house and had several out buildings. One of the buildings looked to be slave quarters.

Jonas and Crockett were very tired so they stopped to see if they may spend the night in one of the buildings. They found out that the man who built this fine house had passed away back in 1834. The man came down the Ohio and started a law office here. John McConnell had served the state in both the house and Senate.

This is the McConnell House and it is still a landmark in the area today.

After his death the big house was converted into a private school. Some of the care takers greeted Jonas and Crockett. They were allowed to sleep in one of the out buildings, and even given some food for supper.

Jonas and Crockett were amazed at the size of the Ohio Valley and how flat the land was. Jonas surmised that farming would be easy in such a place, as he watched several black men and a few whites plow the fields around the big house.

Crockett's Long Trip To Kentucky

"I never seen this many black folks before," Crockett exclaimed.

"I never seen such big fields either," confessed Jonas.

That evening after supper Jonas had Hannah on his mind. He missed the little daughter he left with James and Nancy. He was having second thoughts, and felt bad for leaving her in Virginia. He reasoned within his mind that his decision was right, but it still hurt. She was just too young to travel into the hills of Kentucky with a man and a boy. I will never leave her behind again, Jonas decided.

"What's wrong Paw; you are so quiet this evening?" Crockett asked.

"I have just been thinking about Hannah and the folks back in Virginia," he said.

"I miss them too," Crockett said.

"Don't worry son, we will be all together again, we will build the mills and go back to Hannah," Jonas said.

"Let's get some sleep, we got one long day ahead of us tomorrow," Jonas added.
"Alright paw, do you think we will get there tomorrow?" Crockett asked.

"We have a good shot at it, now get some sleep," Jonas answered.
Next morning as the Whitt's started to move out; the slaves were already at work and singing up a storm. They were singing spiritual songs and enjoying their work.

"Listen to that beautiful singing Crockett," Jonas said.

"I never heard anything like that," said Crockett.

The two moved on down the river and in about half an hour they were coming into Greenup. They could hardly believe they were here already, thinking it was much further to the town.

"Paw is this town of Greenup?" Crockett asked.

"It has to be, I never thought about it being so close to where we stayed last night," Jonas answered.

Crockett's Long Trip To Kentucky

It is a pretty town right on the Ohio River, Jonas thought.

"Looks like it could get flooded out if the river got up big," Jonas said.

Crockett drove the wagon down the main street looking at all the buildings, and businesses. They saw the court house, and a church. It seemed to be a place of tomorrow. There was a landing at the bank of the river just below the court house, and a flat bottomed boat was tied up there. They saw a general store and decided to stop there.

"Let's go in the store and see if we can get directions over to Truittville," Jonas said.

Crockett drove the team up close to the store and got down to tie the team to a hitching post. Jonas led the way into the store where a few people were milling around. Jonas and Crockett walked up to the counter where a clerk was busy adding the cost of another man's purchases.

"Be with you in just a minute," the man said.
"Take your time sir, we just need some directions," Jonas said.

The clerk looked up over his spectacles at Jonas and nodded his head. The clerk finished with the customer, and turned to the strangers in his story.

"Hello there sir my name is James Womack, welcome to Greenupsburg," he said.

"Howdy James, I am Jonas Whitt, this here is my boy David Crockett Whitt, did you say Greenupsburg?" Jonas asked.

"Some of us older settlers still call it that, most new folks call it Greenup," Womack stated.

"We are traveling here from Tazewell County Virginia, and heading to Truittville," Jonas continued.

James shook hands with Jonas and then Crockett.

Crockett's Long Trip To Kentucky

"Good to meet you folks," James said.

"Same here," Jonas said.

"Well Jonas, you said something about directions, where to Truittville?" James asked.

"Yes James, we need to know the best way to get there," Jonas answered.

"Well Jonas it ain't too hard to get too," James said.

James explained the whole trip and directions to Jonas. He told them to go on to the north end of the street; there you will come up on a bridge over the Little Sandy River. Cross the bridge and go on through a little more town. Follow the road about two miles to a little branch. (Coal Branch) Turn up the branch on that road; it takes you over to Tygart Valley. It is slightly up hill for about four miles then the branch runs out at the top of the hill. Another little branch starts at the top and runs to Tygart Creek. It is a decent road after you get over there in the valley. Follow the road south in the valley for about two more miles headed up stream. Next you will come to a big feeder creek. This is Big White Oak Creek. Cross the creek at the ford, and turn up the creek. You will be in Truittville in another three or four mile.

"Sounds good," Jonas said.

"I sure am beholding to you James," Jonas said.

"Do you think we can make it there before dark?" Jonas asked.

"I think you can be there in about two and a half hours on a good riding horse," he said.

"We will be riding in a heavy wagon, and can't go too fast," Jonas explained.

"I think you might make it before dark Jonas, but don't hold me too it," James said.

Jonas bought a plug of tobacco and a stick of candy for Crockett and thanked

Crockett's Long Trip To Kentucky

James Womack for the help.

Jonas told Crockett that they would push on toward Truittville, and would only stop to water the animals. He told Crockett they could eat trail food, since they had a good breakfast.

"We can chew on beef jerky, parched corn, and some dried apples that we brought with us," Jonas said.

Fine with me, I want to hurry up and get there, don't you paw?" Crockett asked.

"Yes I do, we have been on the road for about six weeks now," Jonas replied.

"Has it been that long Paw?" Crockett asked.

"Yelp, we left the last day of March, and today is the tenth of May," Jonas explained.

"Tenth of May, ain't this corn and bean planting day?" Crockett said.

"It sure is, if we were planting, but we are going to build a mill this summer," Jonas said.

Before they knew it they had reached the branch and road that James told them to turn on to.

"This has got to be it," Jonas said.
    Crockett turned the team up the hollow toward Tygart's Valley.

"Paw, we will have to really get on it to make it today, I think we got a good ten miles to go, and it is getting on towards noon," Crockett said.

"I may have bit off more than we can chew for one day," Jonas answered.

"The way this road looks we will be lucky to get a crossed it today," Jonas added.

"Just take your time, if we do we do, if we don't we don't," Jonas surmised.

Crockett's Long Trip To Kentucky

"Like you said Paw, we been a traveling for six weeks, one more day won't matter," Crockett said.

"This hollow reminds me of back in Pike County, except the hills ain't as high," Jonas said.

It was uphill for about four miles; so Crockett let the team pull at their own pace. The grade was not steep until they got close to the one big hill that divided the Ohio and Tygart Valleys.

Once up on the crest of the hill they could look over into Tygart Valley. Crockett stopped on the top for a minute to observe the beautiful valley below them.

"This is a fine land," Jonas thought out loud.

"Paw, we still got about seven miles to go, what time is it?" Crockett asked.

Jonas reached down and pulled out his watch, and flipped open the cover.
"We ain't going to make it today, it's almost 4:00 O'clock, Jonas said.

"Let's travel on over close to Tygart Creek and make camp, the team needs water and food," Jonas said.

It took them close to an hour to descend the hill and travel across the valley to the creek.

They set up camp, took care of the animals, and explored up and down the bank of Tygart Creek.

"Some deep holes in this creek, want to try our luck fishing?" Jonas asked.

"We might as well," Crockett answered.

They were camped at a long deep pool, which reminded them of Grand Paw's Honey Hole back on the Clinch.

Jonas got the fishing poles out while Crockett flipped over rocks and logs for bait.

Crockett's Long Trip To Kentucky

They baited up and sit down to see what they may catch.

Something hit Crockett's hook first, it was a little Bass about ten inches long.

As Crockett allowed it to do a little fighting a great fish rolled up out of the shadows, and took the bass for his dinner. The great fish nearly yanked Crockett's pole from his hand. The fishing line stretched tight and snapped back on the bank. The hook was still there with only a head of a bass still attached.

The big eyed boy turned to Jonas who was also big eyed.

"Paw what on earth was that big thing that stole my fish?" Crockett uttered.

"I have no idea, cept it looked like a pike, I have read about them," Jonas answered excitedly.

"When that thing rolled over it looked to be four feet long," Crockett said.

"I know, I seen it too," replied Jonas.

"Paw, don't fall into this creek, them things might eat you up!" Crockett exclaimed.

"I doubt they would eat a man, but might a boy," Jonas said grinning.

"I don't want to catch that feller," Crockett said.

"Don't worry, I doubt it will strike again," Jonas answered.

They didn't get another bite, so they went back to the camp to find something else for supper. They talked all evening about the trip, about the destination, and about that great fish that took Crockett's fish.

While they were sitting by their camp fire a man road up on his horse.

"Hello in the camp," said the stranger.

"Hello," answered Jonas as he put his hand on his pistol.

Crockett's Long Trip To Kentucky

The man on the horse was a young man of about thirty years.

"I am Alfred Thompson, headed to Truittville," he said.

"I am Jonas Whitt and this here is my boy Crockett," Jonas said.

"Jonas Whitt, are you the one coming to build a mill for Doctor Truitt?" Alfred asked.

"Yes I am, how would you know about that?" Jonas asked.

"Shoot! It is the talk of the county Jonas, we been looking for you for a month," Alfred answered.

"Glad to meet you Jonas and you too Crockett," Alfred added.

"I got some more riding ahead of me so I better get a going," Alfred said.

"Wait just a minute, can you tell me how far it is?" Jonas asked.

"About four or five miles I reckon," answered Alfred.

"How is the road on in to Truittville?" Jonas asked.

"It is a fine road on in to Truittville," he answered.

"Well thank you Alfred, do you need a drink of water or a bite to eat?" Jonas asked.
"No sir, I will be fine till I get to the Truitt Inn," Alfred said.

"Thank you Jonas for the offer, I will tell the Truitt's to expect you all tomorrow afternoon," Alfred said as he headed up the road at a good gait.

"Paw they must be excited about us coming," Crockett said.

"Reckon so, I guess we will be in demand to build them a grist mill," Jonas answered.

Crockett's Long Trip To Kentucky

"Paw I was going to ask that feller about that fish we saw, but I couldn't get a word in," Crockett said.

"Don't worry about it son you will have plenty of time to ask about the big pike, we better get some sleep, so we can get on in to Truittville, Jonas said.

"Alright paw," Crockett said as he pulled his big quilt up around his neck.

"Good night son," Jonas answered.

Alfred Thompson made it into Truittville about an hour after dark. He told Louisa Truitt, Samuel's daughter that the mill builder is only a few hours away. She ran to the Family home and aroused them. Samuel wanted to know what is going on. She told them that Alfred Thompson just rode in, and had talked to the Whitt's over on Tygart.

"Glory be, we are going to get us a mill yet," Samuel said.

"I will ride out in the morning to meet Jonas and his son, Polly ain't you excited?" Samuel asks his sleepy wife.

"Sure am, now can we go to sleep?" Polly asked.

"Thanks Louisa for bringing the news, now go back and take care of our guests at the Inn," Samuel said.

"Good night Louisa," he added.

"Good night Paw, good night Maw," Louisa said.

Next morning Jonas and Crockett was up early, had a quick breakfast, and was moving toward Truittville. The excitement and anticipation were building for Jonas and Crockett. Even the mules and Jake were feeling the excitement that flowed from Jonas and Crockett. The mules trotted like fine horses as they pulled the wagon up the Tygart Valley. Before long the Whitt's reached the mouth of Big White Oak Creek.

Crockett's Long Trip To Kentucky

"This has to be it," Jonas said.

"Over there is the fording place, see the wagon tracks heading into the creek?" Crockett asked.

"Go ahead and go to it, just go slow through the water," Jonas cautioned.

The creek was clear and had a rock bottom, so it was an ideal spot to ford.

"This is a beautiful creek," Jonas said.

"Reckon there is any of them great fish like we saw yesterday in here?" Crockett asked.

"I doubt that something that big would come up the creek, but you never know," answered Jonas.

The team took them out of the water and up on a rolling hill, which presented the valley to them. The road was heavily used. They could tell this by the numerous wagon tracks and horse tracks.

As they traveled up the valley, they marveled at this picturesque landscape.

They passed two wagons and one man on horseback, also two boys carrying fishing poles toward the creek.

Most of the leaves were on the trees, and folks were here and there planting the fields and gardens. Jonas and Crockett were in awe at what their eyes beheld.

"Paw this is a fine place, this Big White Oak Valley," Crockett said.
"It sure is, it is much more beautiful than I expected," Jonas said.

As they traveled up the valley another couple miles they saw a buggy come over a rise in the road. It was making good time they noticed.

"Paw here comes a buggy and it is coming lickety-split," Crockett announced.

"I see it son, wonder what the hurry is?" Jonas asked.

Crockett's Long Trip To Kentucky

In about two more minutes the buggy pulled up beside the Whitt wagon. The driver was an older plump man, and the passenger was a handsome woman in her early twenties.

"Hello there," the older man said.

"Are you Jonas Whitt?" he asked before Jonas could speak.

"Yes sir, I am Jonas and this here is my son David Crockett Whitt," Jonas answered.

"Glad to meet you gentlemen, I am Samuel Truitt and this is my daughter Mildred we call her Millie," Samuel said.

"Glad to meet you sir and your daughter," Jonas said as he tipped his hat toward Millie.

Millie gave them a beautiful smile, as did the gentleman Dr. Samuel Truitt.
"We been looking for you for about a month," Samuel said.

"We have been traveling since the last day of March, had to go slow with this heavy wagon," Jonas explained.

"I brought all my tools, and a few farming implements, plus traveling gear," Jonas added.

"Well you fellers are a sight for sore eyes, I mean that in a good way Mister Whitt," Samuel stated.

"I know what you mean Mister Truitt, I feel the same way about seeing you and Miss Truitt," Jonas said.

"Mister Whitt, how about you calling me Sam?" Samuel said.

"Fine sir, please call me Jonas, after all we will be seeing a lot of each other," Jonas answered.

Crockett's Long Trip To Kentucky

"Well Jonas, the longer we sit here, the longer it will be before you get to your purpose," Samuel said.

"I will turn this buggy around and get back to the Inn, and get ready for you and young Crockett," he said as he circled the Whitt wagon.

"How much further is it Sam?" Jonas asked.

"You will be there in about an hour, just stop at the Inn right beside the road," Samuel instructed.

"Thanks Sam, we will be there dreckly," Jonas said.

The speedy buggy moved out of sight once again. Crockett drove the team up through the valley at a little accelerated speed. Jonas and Crockett talked about this new land in Greenup County Kentucky. They talked about Dr. Samuel Truitt, and even mentioned his lovely daughter Mildred. Before they knew it they had talked themselves the last mile of the way. There ahead was a big two story Inn, also there was a big family house and several other buildings. One little building had a sign reading "Truittville Post Office."

As they pulled up to the Inn, Jonas had a thought of Hannah and those they left behind.

"Tonight or tomorrow, I am going write to Hannah and the rest of our family and let them know we made it here, I will let them know about this place and that they are dearly missed," Jonas said as he looked at the post office.

"That is a good idea, they don't know where we are, what I mean, they don't know if we made it yet," answered Crockett.

"I understand son, they will be glad to get our letter," Jonas said.

"Our letter Paw, does that mean it is from me too?" Crockett asked.

"Of course, the letter will be from you too, you can even write something in it," Jonas answered.

Crockett's Long Trip To Kentucky

By now Samuel, Louisa, and Mildred were greeting them at their wagon.

Samuel was a nice looking gentleman, but a little chubby. He had a round face with no beard, only a nicely trimmed mustache. He spoke in a calm manner with a friendly disposition. He was a proper person with good breeding and upbringing. He made everyone feel at ease in his presence.

Louisa was the daughter that ran the Truitt Inn. She was just opposite of her father. She talked a lot and said what she thought regardless of where the words landed.

Mildred was a handsome lady that smiled at Jonas and Crockett. She did not say much but her feelings could be felt by others.

Samuel took the hand of Jonas and gave him a genuine welcome. And then also shook Crockett's hand. The girls did likewise. Jonas did not want to read anything in it but his heart leaped when he took Millie's hand.

"Did you all have a good trip up from Tazewell County?" Samuel asked.

"Yes sir I think so, but I am glad to have finally reached your home," Jonas answered.

"Well I am glad you all made it without a major problem," Samuel continued.

"Are you gentleman hungry?" Louisa asked.

"Yes Miss Louisa, I think we both could eat," Jonas answered.

There was a man working in the stable that Jonas noticed. Samuel noticed Jonas looking toward the stable. Samuel waved for the man to come over. The man dropped his work on the table by the stable and came to meet Jonas.

"This is Tony Montivon, he makes shoes for our little berg, and does other things to help people," Samuel said.

"Hello there Tony, I am Jonas Whitt, this here is my boy Crockett," Jonas said.

Crockett's Long Trip To Kentucky

"Glad to meet you Jonas, and you Crockett," Tony said in a deep French assent.

"Where are you from Tony?" Jonas asked.

"I am a Frenchman from Canada," he answered.

"Would you like for me to care for your animals while you have your dinner?" Tony asked.

"We can take care of them," Jonas said.

"No, No, Mister Whitt, let me do this for you and young Crockett," Tony said.

"Let him help Jonas, he loves to stay busy," Samuel said.

"Well if you insist," Jonas answered.

Tony went up and took hold of the halter of the lead mule and led them toward the big barn.

Samuel turned to Jonas and Crockett.

"Jonas, let me show you your room and then you and Crockett eat you dinner, take the rest of the day and get settled," Samuel said.

"If you need anything, anything at all don't hesitate to ask," Samuel said as he led Jonas and Crockett into the Inn.

"Now this bottom floor is a tavern and dining area and here is the steps up to the rooms," Samuel said pointing them out.

Jonas noticed that a couple of families were eating and a few single men also. It was a nice Inn for the time and area.

Samuel led Jonas and Crockett up the stairs and to the last room on the left. It had bunk beds, a wash stand, a small desk, and a little iron stove.

"Thank you Samuel this will do just fine," Jonas said.

Crockett's Long Trip To Kentucky

"Welcome Jonas, have you ever used a stove for heat?" Samuel Asked.

"No sir, matter of fact I ain't never seen one, I have heard of them though," Jonas answered.

"It does a fine job, I got one in every room, had them shipped down from Pittsburgh last summer," Samuel explained.

"If you want a bath, just tell Louisa and she will see that you have a tub of hot water prepared," Samuel added.

"I will be around bout supper time and we can talk some," Samuel said as he was heading out the door.

Jonas went over and sits down to try out the bed. Crockett followed him and sits down too.

"Well Crockett, we are here, guess we will have to build Samuel a mill." Jonas said.

"Guess so paw, when will we start?" Crockett asked.

"In the morning son, we will figure it all out in the morning," Jonas answered.

Jonas and Crockett went down by the barn to get some of their things from the wagon. They walked around in the area of the house, barn, and Inn, just taking in the lay of the land. Both of them were getting hungry, so they took their belongings to the Inn. On the way upstairs Jonas told Louisa that they would like something to eat. After dinner Jonas would walk the creek bank and get some ideas where to build the new grist mill.

After eating dinner, and relaxing a spell, Jonas and Crockett got up and headed out to see the Truitt farm.

As they went by the big house, Mary Elizabeth Gibbs (Polly) was sitting on the porch. She waved at Jonas and Crockett to come closer.

"I am Polly, Sam's wife, you must be Mister Whitt," she said.

Crockett's Long Trip To Kentucky

"Yes ma-am, I am Jonas, this here is Crockett my boy," he said.

"Well Jonas you call me Polly, everybody else does," Polly said.

"I want to welcome you and Crockett to our place, just make yourself to home," she added.

"Thank you Polly, we are out stretching our legs and are going to look at the creek," Jonas answered.

About that time Mildred came out of the house and waved at Jonas and Crockett.

"Hello Miss Mildred," Jonas said.

Crockett tipped his hat, but didn't say anything!

"Millie, Jonas and Crockett are going on a walk to see the property, would you mind walking with them and showing them around?" Polly asked.

"I will be glad to show them around if Mister Whitt would like," Mildred said.

"Call me Jonas, and we would be glad for you to show us around," Jonas answered.

Mildred joined Jonas and Crockett on their walk about. She pointed out the Post Office, the little shoe factory that Tony ran. She pointed to a few other cabins and told Jonas who lived in them. They walked down by Big White Oak Creek, so that Jonas could get some ideas as to where to build the new mill.

"This is a purty farm, and everything Miss Mildred," Crockett said.

"Well thank you Crockett, we try to be self-sufficient, Paw is the Post Master, Medical Doctor, Engineer, Farmer, and School Teacher, she said.

"The one big thing we lack in Truittville is a Grist Mill," Mildred added.

Crockett's Long Trip To Kentucky

"Me and Paw will fix you one of them," Crockett said.
"I know you will, and that will help a lot of people," She said.

"I meant the purty hills and this little valley when I said purty farm," Crockett said.

"Yes, we love our hills here in Greenup, County," Mildred answered.

Jonas went down close to the creek and inspected every aspect of it as they walked. The farm was laid out on mostly level ground with a rise on the upper end. The level areas by the creek were well kept and mostly treeless.

"Do you ever have floods that get out of the banks?" Jonas asked.

"Never has yet, but it does get up sometimes, and in the hot part of summer it gets down kinda low," she said.

"That is good to know, there may not be any grinding when the creek gets low, most people do their milling in the fall and winter anyway," Jonas stated.

"Looks like the creek bottom is mostly rock," Jonas added.

"What about fish Miss Mildred, are there any fish in this creek?" Crockett asked.

"Sure is, we catch Red Eyes, and some Small Mouth Bass in the bigger holes," she answered.
This brought a wide grin to Crockett's face.

"Go ahead and ask her Crockett," Jonas said.

"Miss Mildred, I was fishing yesterday evening in Tygart, and a giant fish bit my bass right into," Crockett explained.

"Muskie, you had a Muskie after you're bass, I have seen some about four feet long," she answered.

"Will they eat people?" Crockett asked.

"Never heard of it," she said laughing.

Crockett's Long Trip To Kentucky

"My Paw caught one about three feet long one time, it's mouth was full of teeth, folks come from all around to fish for them, you have to use a wire at the end of your line to fasten your hook on it because of the teeth," Mildred explained.

Crockett looked at Jonas and grinned real big.

"I guess you want to go after one?" Jonas asked.

"When we get the mill done, we might have time, huh paw?" Crockett asked.

"We will see Son, we will get the mill built as soon as possible," Jonas said.

"Miss Mildred, where could I get some letter writing materials?" Jonas asked.

"Paw keeps some around the Post Office," she replied.

"I bet your folks back home are anxious to hear from you, especially your wife," Mildred said.

"Yes my little girl Hannah is staying with my brother James and his wife, my dear wife passed about eight years ago," Jonas said.

"So sorry to hear that Jonas," replied Mildred.

"Thanks Miss Mildred, we better get back and get settled in I guess," Jonas said.

Crockett's Long Trip To Kentucky

Chapter 7
Building A Mill In Truittville.

Jonas and Crockett headed to the Post Office on the way back to the Inn. By now it was getting close to supper time and Jonas wanted to write that letter to Hannah and the rest of the family.

Just as they got to the post office, Samuel Truitt was just coming out. Samuel was the post master and he worked about an hour a day in the little Office. The post rider only come by on Monday and Thursday, to bring mail and take it back to Greenup and South Shore. Greenup was a bigger Post Office and sent mail out by boat, wagon, and riders, as did South Shore. South Shore lay across the Ohio River from Portsmouth Ohio.

"Hello Jonas and you too Crockett, do you have some mailing to do?" asked Samuel.

"Just looking for some letter writing materials, so we can write the folks back home," Jonas said.

"I will get you some stationary and envelopes, then I am heading over to get Polly, we eat most of our meals in the Inn," explained Samuel.

Samuel gave Jonas a few sheets of paper and a couple of envelopes, and locked the door to the Post Office.

"Jonas I will see you all at the Inn, after supper we will talk about building me a mill, if that is all right with you?" Samuel asked.

"That will be fine, a feller thinks better on a full belly," Jonas said.

Samuel headed over to his big house to escort Polly to supper. Jonas and Crockett headed back to their room to put away their papers and get ready for supper.

"We will write that letter soon as we can get back from supper, remember me and Mister Truitt have some business first," Jonas exclaimed.

Crockett's Long Trip To Kentucky

"Paw I seen a calendar at the post office, this is Tuesday the eleventh, that means the mail goes out day after tomorrow," Crockett said.

"Don't worry son the letter will go with the post carrier on Thursday," Jonas answered.

"Are you going to write something in it?" Jonas asked.

"I reckon I will, I don't want anybody forgetting me," Crockett said.

"They ain't likely to forget you Crockett," Jonas said laughing.

Jonas and Crockett went to their room, laid their paper on the little desk that Sam had provided. Then they washed their hands and headed down for supper.

Louisa ask where they would like to be seated, and took them to a table by a window. She brought them both a plate of steaming beef stew, corn bread, and hot tea to drink. She also told them about deserts.

They had just started to eat when they noticed Samuel and Polly come in the door. Samuel and Polly both gave Jonas and Crockett a wave. Jonas and Crockett waved back and kept eating. Samuel and Polly both sat at a table in the corner which had a little sign on it, reading reserved.

"That must be the Truitt's favorite table Paw," Crockett whispered.

Jonas nodded his head at Crockett.

After a leisurely meal topped off with apple cobbler, Crockett and his Paw were full to the brim.

"What are you going to do while me and Mister Truitt talk business?" Jonas asked.

"If you don't mind I think I will go up and write my letter," Crockett answered.

"That will be fine, but will you bring that case of my mill drawings down to me first?" Jonas asked.

Crockett's Long Trip To Kentucky

"Sure will, is it with your clothes bag?" Crockett asked.

"I set it right beside the desk, you can't miss it," Jonas said.

Crockett was up the steps and back in quick time.

"This is it, ain't it Paw?" Crockett asked.

"Sure is son, now go write your letter, I will be up dreckly," Jonas said.

"If you get bored you can go out and look around, just don't interrupt me and Mister Truitt," Jonas exclaimed.

"Don't worry Paw, I know not to brother you when you do business," Crockett said.

"Good boy," Jonas answered.

Jonas spread out some of his drawings on the table so he could explain mill workings to Samuel Truitt.

Samuel helped Polly up from the table, gave her a little kiss, and told her he would be home after Jonas and he were finished talking business.

Crockett went upstairs to write his letter.

Mister Truitt lit a cigar and offered one to Jonas.

"I will take one for later Sam, I will do better explaining this stuff without smoking," Jonas answered.

Jonas dug out an old drawing of a bottom shot grist mill, and turned it so that Sam could see it.

"Sam this is the mill that we will build, it is the best type for the creek and terrain I have observed here," Jonas said.

Sam just sit and studied the drawing as Jonas explained.

Crockett's Long Trip To Kentucky

"It looks complicated," Samuel said.

"It can be, but it will all make sense to you later," Jonas answered.

"Miss Mildred showed me the creek and the land this afternoon, and I feel this is the best type to build here," Jonas continued.

"I think up the creek just below the little knoll, will be a good place to build it," Jonas said.

"How do you get the water to it?" Samuel asked.

"That is a good question, it will involve the most work of the whole thing," Jonas said.

"We will build the mill thirty to forty feet off the creek, and dig a trace off the creek to the wheel," Jonas pointed out.

"Now do you have people to help dig the trace?" Jonas asked.

"We can get the labor for that, what else do we need to think about Jonas?" Samuel asked.

"Well Sir, we need lumber for the building that houses the mill, we need red wood for the wheel, and we need timbers to hold up the great weight of the mill works." Jonas said.

"We will need some Iron brackets, and hardware, Oh! Yes we will have to acquire two mill wheels," Jonas continued.

"Granite is best material to make grinding wheels from, but hard to get, so limestone will work," Jonas explained.

"My brother Richard, lives down in Carter County, you know the man that told you about me, he said they had plenty of limestone in that area," Jonas said.

"Yes I remember Richard, is he a stone cutter?" Samuel asked.

Crockett's Long Trip To Kentucky

"That is not a regular trade for him, but he has cut stone before," Jonas answered.

Samuel looked at the drawing again, and scratched his head.

"That Alfred Thompson that you met on the trail is a fine lumber man, he will fill your order for the boards, and timbers" Samuel said.

"What about foundation stone, I think we can get that out of the creek and out of the ground we dig, do you think that will work?" Samuel asked.

"I would think so," Jonas answered.

"Samuel, do you have limestone or Granite about, and do you know a stone cutter?" Jonas asked.

"Well I will have to think about that," Samuel said.

"I can cut them out, but it will expedite things if I can order them and spend my time building the mill," Jonas said.

"Do you think Richard Whitt can provide the mill stones?" Samuel asked.

"I think he could," replied Jonas.

"Just off the top of your head Jonas, how long do you think it will take to get her built?" Samuel asked.

"Too many factors, but I would give a wild guess of about a year to a year and a half," Jonas answered.

"That is about what I guessed," Samuel surmised.

"Here Jonas explain this drawing, I see the big water wheel, do you have to make the gears to turn the stone grinding wheel?" Samuel asked.

"Yes I have to build it all, the water wheel, the big gear, the little gear and the shafts, shoots and make it all adjustable," Jonas said.

Jonas explained the workings but did not share all the secrets of mill building with Samuel. If everyone knew how to build a mill, Who would need a mill-right, Jonas thought.

"I will go out and start laying out the earth works and do some planning in the morning, I have a material list," Jonas said.

"That will be great," Samuel said.

"I will come by and see what you need, but don't worry I will let you be fully in charge, that is what I hired you for," Samuel said.

"I am a might tired Samuel, would you excuse me, I want to write that letter before I retire," Jonas said.

"Of course you are tired, I am just anxious to have a mill, you go and take care of things and I will see you sometime in the morning," Samuel answered.

"By the way Jonas, my stable man is taking care of your mules and saddle horse for you," Samuel said.

"Thank you so much Sam I thought you were; see you on the morrow Sam," Jonas said.

Jonas went up the steps to his room, wondering if Crockett finished his letter.

As Jonas came in the room, Crockett was sitting at the desk still writing on his letter.

"You still writing on your letter Crockett?" Jonas asked.

"Yes sir, I had to decide what to write and then figure out how to spell some of the words," Crockett answered.

"Well son the spelling is not that important to family, long as they can make it out," Jonas said.

Crockett's Long Trip To Kentucky

"Good thing Paw," Crockett answered.

"Are you about done?" he asked.
"Just got to sign my name Paw," Crockett answered.

"Would you like to read it and check it over for me?" Crockett asked.

"I can if you don't mind me knowing what you wrote," Jonas said.

Crockett gave the letter to Jonas to read. Jonas sits down on the bed and read the letter.

Dear Hannah, Uncle James and the hole family.
Me and Paw got here in Truittville today may 11, and it is a purty place. The Truitts are good people I think. Sam is a rich man. Mildred his girl likes me and Paw. We have a orn stove in our room.
They are big fish in Tygart creek that are so big one bit my bass into. We had a purty good trip I reckon. Seen some necked women, a man got hung, us and the mules rode a boat a cross vicy river. Me and paw had to stand off a outlaw, and some Fleming fellows. We stopped and seen Uncle John in floyd county. We gonna start building the mill tomorrow. I luv you Hannah, Elizabeth, Emma, James Griffy, John , Rachel, Rhoda, and all your families. We miss you so much and you to uncle James and aint Nancy.
Yours truly   David Crockett Whitt

Jonas smiled as he hands the letter back to Crockett.

"Is it alright Paw?" Crockett asked.

"It will be fine," Jonas replied.

Jonas thought to himself, what questions the folks back home would have after reading Crockett's letter.

"Paw did you and Mister Truitt have a good meeting about the mill?" Crockett asked.

Crockett's Long Trip To Kentucky

"I think so, we are going to lay out some of the work in the morning, and make more plans," Jonas explained.

"It is about to get dark, do you need to go out and visit the Johnny before bed?" Jonas asked.

"I might ort to," Crockett answered.

Jonas sit down to collect his thoughts and put them into his letter home.

This is what he wrote:

May 11, 1847
    Truitt Inn, Truittville, Greenup County, Kentucky
    Dear Hannah, James, Nancy and Family,
    It has been a hard trip, but we made it just fine. We arrived this afternoon and have already got plans to build the mill for Doctor Samuel Truitt. We are fine but are a little tired. We had no great problems on the trip, but it was an adventure.
    We spent two days with Brother John Bunyon over in Floyd County. They were doing fine.
    I intend to get the new grist mill built expediently so Crockett and I can return home to you. I now wonder if I did the right thing leaving little Hannah there. I know she is being cared for and is not subject to dangers of travel. I truly miss her as does Crockett. We miss all of you.
    This is a pretty land and the people are good from all that I can tell. We have a nice room in the Truitt Inn. As Crockett mentioned in his letter, we have an iron stove for heat. The food is good in the tavern down stairs.
    Crockett and I are both well and ready for the challenge of building the mill. We hope to be on our way back home next spring, Lord permitting.
    How is everyone doing in Tazewell County? Please write us letters and keep us informed as to happenings, and your lives.
    I hope to visit Brother Richard in Carter County about a day's ride from here, while we are here.
    Hannah and family we love you! Write soon.
      Love you. Jonas Whitt

Jonas took Crockett's letter and put it with his, he folded them and put them in

Crockett's Long Trip To Kentucky

the envelope. Jonas wrote the address on the envelope, Hannah Whitt, C/O James Whitt, Kentucky Turnpike, Tazewell County, Virginia. Next he dropped some candle wax on it to seal it.

"Well Crockett it is ready to take to the post office," Jonas said.

Crockett was lying in the top bunk, and looked at his Paw.

"Paw do we still have to pay the postage when we give it to Mister Truitt?" Crockett asked.

"Some time tomorrow I will take it in the post office and pay the postage, then Thursday it will go out with the rider," Jonas exclaimed.

"I can't believe we finally got here, can you paw?" Crockett asked.

"It has been a long trip, but we are here and start work tomorrow," Jonas said.

"I am blowing out the lamp, you go to sleep, I will see you in the morning," Jonas said.

"Good night Paw, don't forget to pray your prayers," Crockett said.

"I will pray out loud, right now so you will know I prayed," Jonas said.

Jonas begins his prayer: *"Dear Heavenly Father, we give thanks for your loving kindness, and watch care over your servants. Lord we thank you for bringing us to this new land safely. We pray for our loved ones we left at home, Lord Watch over them and keep them safe we pray. Lord we pray for your wisdom and strength to build the mill for Mister Truitt. We ask a blessing on this new land and help us to be your true servants. Dear Lord we pray for the forgiveness of our sins and short comings. Lord we pray that when you are done with us that you will take us unto your bosom and into the promised rest of your Heaven. We ask this in the name of Jesus Christ, Amen."*

Crockett fell asleep with a smile on his face. They both slept well and woke to a nice Kentucky May day. The weather was warm and no sign of rain was seen.

Crockett's Long Trip To Kentucky

"Good morning Crockett, you ready to go and start that mill?" Jonas asked.

"Well I guess so, soon as I can get woke up," Crockett answered.

"We can go down and eat some breakfast and wake up on some coffee," Jonas answered.

Jonas and Crockett jumped in their overalls and hooked their galleasses, washed their faces and hands and were ready for the day. They headed down stairs into the eatery.

Louisa was carrying a pot of coffee to each table. She looked up to see Jonas and Crockett coming to eat.

"Good morning Jonas, and you too Crockett," Louisa said.

"Good morning to you Miss Louisa," Jonas said.

"Morning Ma-ma," Crockett said as he headed to the table by the window.

"Coffee?" Louisa asked?

"Yes, a cup for both of us please," Jonas answered.

The dining area was full of folks this morning. Men ready for a day's work and some ladies also. Some of them were people only spending the night at Truitt's Inn.

Louisa brought the Whitt's coffee, and told them that she had a big skillet of gravy, and some Cathead biscuits.

"I can fix you some bust eggs too," she added.

"Two eggs a piece and some of that Kentucky gravy and biscuits will be just fine," Jonas said.

Jonas and Crockett enjoyed their breakfast, and headed to their wagon to get some items needed to lay out the mill. Crockett also went over and seen Jake and

Crockett's Long Trip To Kentucky

the Mules. Bill Thompson (William Randolph Thompson) was working in the big barn caring for the livestock.

"I am Bill Thompson, I work for Doctor Truitt, you must be the Whitt's," Bill said.

"That's right Bill," Jonas answered.

"I am Jonas and this is my son, Crockett," Jonas continued.

"I been taking care of your mules and that fine saddle horse for you, do you want them turned out in the field?" Bill asked.

"Thank you so much Bill that will be fine, we have to get some twine, a measuring tape, a hatchet out of the wagon, and get to work," Jonas said.

"Doctor Truitt told me to follow along and do whatever you need me to do," Bill said.

"I didn't know Bill, that will be a heap of help," Jonas answered.

Jonas and Crockett got the tools and headed up the creek to the rise in the creek bank. Bill finished up and let the animals loose into the big pasture, next he followed Jonas and Crockett up the creek.

Jonas and Crockett laid down the tools about thirty feet from the creek.

Jonas walked over to the creek with Crockett and Bill following right behind him. Jonas looked up and down the creek. He scratched his head and spit out a shot of amber. He turned to look at Bill and Crockett.

"At the lower end of that little hole is where we will build the dam, want a chew, Bill?" Jonas asked.

"Got some Jonas," Bill answered.

"What are you going to use to build the dam with?" Bill asked.

"Mostly rocks," Jonas said.

Crockett's Long Trip To Kentucky

"It don't have to hold back all the water, just enough to convert it through the trace," Jonas explained.

"Trace, what trace?" Bill asked.

"The one we are going to dig from the creek to the mill and back to the creek," Jonas answered.

"I need for you to sharpen me some stakes about two foot long," Jonas said to Bill.

"Bout how many you needing Jonas?" Bill asked.

"About two dozen I reckon, Crockett go with Bill up in the edge of the woods and help cut some of them saplings for stakes," Jonas instructed.

Bill and Crockett headed up the rise and Jonas walked up and down the creek bank looking it over.

Jonas got out the drawing of the mill and looked it over again, gathering the thoughts that would someday transverse into a two story mill with water flowing swiftly under the twenty foot wheel and grinding grain. He carried the paper to the edge of the creek again and looked at the creek and back at the drawing.

Next Jonas stepped off about fifteen paces straight from the creek. He dug in his right heel to mark the spot. This will be where the water wheel will set, thought Jonas.

Crockett comes down off the hill with an arm load of stakes, and Bill Thompson continued to cut more stakes.

"Paw, did you say stakes or snakes?" Crockett asked.

"Stakes, don't want no snakes," Jonas answered.

"Bill kilt a copperhead right beside a sapling he was cuttun," Crockett said.

"My goodness, did it strike at him?" Jonas asked.

Crockett's Long Trip To Kentucky

"It bit his hatchet, and then Bill hacked it in two," Crockett said.

"Thank God it didn't bite you all," Jonas said.

"That reminds me of a story," Jonas said.

"About the rattle snake a biting the log Paw?" Crockett asked.

"Yelp, I will tell it to Bill when he gets back here," Jonas said.

Bill Thompson is back with another arm load of stakes.

"Crockett tell you bout that copperhead Jonas?" Bill asked.
"Yes he did, that sounded like a close call for you," Jonas answered.

"Kinda was," Bill said.

"It reminds me of when a feller back home was logging," Jonas said.

"What happened Jonas?" Bill asked?

Well Bill, the fellers name was John; he cut out a nice ten foot log about a foot through it. He went over to put a chain on it to drag it to the saw mill and there was a giant Timber Rattler. That ole snake reared back and struck at John but missed and bit the log.

"What happened next?" Bill asked.

"Well John came down on that rattler with his double bit ax and whacked off his head," Jonas continued.

"What went on next?" Bill asked.

"Well Bill that log began to swell and it got about twenty five foot long and about four foot thick," Jonas answered.

"What on earth did John do with it then?" Bill asked.
    "He got four yoke of oxen and drug it to the saw mill and cut it into fine

lumber, and built himself a fine barn," Jonas continued.

"My goodness Jonas, is that all of the story?" Bill asked.

"Nope, in about three days the swelling went out and John had himself a nice chicken coop, it was a good thing he didn't have his horses in it," Jonas said with a grin.

Bill laid back and hollered and laughed.

"You really had me going for a while Jonas, that is a real good story," Bill exclaimed.

"Well we better get to work, this mill ain't gonna build itself," Jonas said.

Jonas showed Crockett where he had marked the ground with his heel.

"Put a stake right here and drive it in straight, leave about a foot of sticking out," Jonas instructed.

Crockett drove in the stake and stood up for more instructions.

Jonas got out his tape measure and handed one end to Bill.

"Here Bill, hold it on the stake, please," Jonas said.

As Bill held the end of the tape Jonas stretched it out parallel with the creek to a length of eight feet.

"Here Crockett drive in another stake," Jonas said.

Crockett drove it in straight and left about a foot above the ground just like the other.

"That is fine son," Jonas said.

"Now Bill would you hold it on this stake?" Jonas asked.

Crockett's Long Trip To Kentucky

As Bill held it on the second stake Jonas moved in another direction, straight away from the creek to another eight feet. Jonas squatted down and eyeballed the line to the stake.

"Stake right here Crockett," Jonas said.

Crockett moved to the spot and sunk another stake, straight and true.

"Alright Bill, hold it here on this stake please," Jonas instructed.

"Crockett let me have one of them stakes, Jonas said.

Jonas took the stake, stretched the tape to eight feet back in the downstream direction and marked the spot with an arch drawn with the stake.

"Bill move to the first stake again and hold it for me," Jonas instructed.

Bill moved the tape to the first stake and Jonas stretched the tape measure to eight feet away from the creek to the arch he scribed in the ground. Jonas took the stake again and scribed out another arch across the first arch.

"Stake it right here Crockett, right at the cross of the two arches," Jonas instructed.

After Crockett sank the fourth stake, Jonas had Bill hold the tape measure on one stake as he measured straight across from corner to corner. Then he had Bill move eight feet to the next stake. Once again Jonas measured straight across corner to corner. Jonas pulled the last stake and moved it about two inches. Then he moved the next stake about two inches.

"Alright Bill lets measure from corner to corner again," Jonas said.
"Paw, you are squaring it up, ain't you?" Crockett asked.

"Yelp, trying to," Jonas answered.

Bill held the tape again and then on the opposite corner just like before.

"Great that is real close," Jonas said with a smile.

Crockett's Long Trip To Kentucky

"I wondered what we were doing measuring back and forth corner to corner," Bill said.

"I ain't never seen nobody square up something before," he added.

"This is where the water wheel will sit," Jonas exclaimed.

"Right cher?" Bill asked.

"That's right Bill," Jonas answered.

"We must be forty, fifty foot off the creek," Bill exclaimed.

"I know, we are going to bring the creek to the mill," Jonas said.

"Alright Jonas, you are the mill builder, I will be quiet," Bill said.

"That is alright, you may ask a question any time you want," Jonas answered.

Next Jonas, Bill, and Crockett laid out a trace to come into the creek just above the proposed dam. They staked it all out as they stretched a line to make it straight and true.

As they were laying out the return trace away from the water wheel area back to the creek, Doctor Samuel Truitt and Millie came over to talk to Jonas.

"Hello Sam and you too Miss Mildred," Jonas said.

"Good day to you gentleman," Samuel answered.

"Please call me Millie, Jonas and you too Crockett," Millie said with a smile.

"Well good day Miss Millie," Jonas answered.

"Hello Miss Millie," Crockett said sheepishly.

Samuel told them he was on his way over to the post office to do a little work and

Crockett's Long Trip To Kentucky

thought he would ask how things were going. Jonas showed Samuel the work that was already laid out, and pointed out the spot the water wheel would be. "Plumb over here," Samuel exclaimed.

"We are going to bring the water to it Mister Truitt," Bill Thompson explained.

Jonas and Crockett looked at Bill and smiled.

"Alright men, you are the mill-rights, not me," Samuel said.

"Jonas have you got a material lists ready yet?" Samuel asked.
Yes sir, it is all written out here in my book, as I said before we are going to build this undershot mill in the drawing," Jonas explained.

"I will let you borrow this book for a day and you can scribe you out a copy, or have Miss Millie do it for you," Jonas suggested.

"Alright I can do that, you show Millie what needs written out if you would," Samuel said.

"Just as soon as we get done with our talk I will show Millie what we need scribed out," Jonas answered.

I have been thinking about the grinding stones Sam, Granite is the very best stone to cut them out of," Jonas said.

"We could order them and have them shipped to us at a later date while we do the other work," Jonas said.

"What about the limestone wheels from your brother?" Sam asked.

"We can get them, but limestone is softer than granite and must be dressed much more often," Jonas answered.

"Well Jonas do you have a place in mind to order them from?" Samuel asked.

"The very best, but most costly come from Italy, the Gerardi Family in Pittsburgh deal in importing them," Jonas explained.

Crockett's Long Trip To Kentucky

"They usually keep a set and can ship as soon as they receive payment," Jonas explained.

"Do we really need two grinding stones Jonas?" Samuel asked.

"Yes sir, a set stone and a turn stone," Jonas explained.

"How much would it take to get two stones delivered to South Shore or Greenup?" Samuel asked.

"Now Sam this will be the most costly purchase for the mill, I can make everything else except for some hardware," Jonas said.

"How much Jonas," Samuel asked?

"I would think between one hundred fifty and two hundred dollars, including shipping them down the Ohio," Jonas said.

"That is expensive Jonas, but I want something that will last and require less maintenance, let's get them ordered.

"Best way would be having the bank draft them a check for one hundred dollars and pay the rest when they arrive," Jonas said.

"You may add my name as the mill-right since I have dealt with them before," Jonas added.

"Jonas you get a drawing and description of the stones ready and write out the requirements, sign your name at the bottom and I will get them ordered," Samuel instructed.

"I will have it ready for the postman tomorrow Sam," Jonas said.

"By the way do you have your letters ready to mail?" Samuel asked.

"Now Samuel we are just about ready to dig and I want to build a storage building here near by the mill," Jonas explained.

Crockett's Long Trip To Kentucky

"Alright Jonas I will get you some labor to do the digging, my brother over in Lewis County has eight servants he will contract out," Samuel said.

"Also I will get with Alfred Thompson and have him start getting your lumber to you," Samuel continued.

"Sounds good, we will be grinding grain before you know it," Jonas said.

"Do you have someone in mind to be your miller?" Jonas asked.

"William Randolph Thompson, that is why I put him with you from the ground up," Samuel said.

"Now Sam, I will not have Millie copy the hardware list, I intend having Richard Whitt fabricate it in his blacksmith shop, if that is alright with you?" Jonas asked.

"Long as he is fair and does a good job, I will leave that to you," Samuel said.

Millie took the book and asked Jonas to explain and point out what had to be copied. Jonas explained in a real soft voice as he enjoyed being close to Millie.

"Jonas have you got time to sit on the porch with me for a minute, and make sure I know what to copy?" Millie asked.

Samuel headed to the Post Office.

Jonas sent Crockett to their room to get the letters and take them to the post office, and he headed to the porch with Millie Truitt.

Crockett's Long Trip To Kentucky

Chapter 8

Jonas Falls In Love!

Jonas points out all that needs to be copied. Then he dictates another small list that he wants first. The last list of material will be for a shed to store things in and a place to get in out of the weather while the mill is under construction.

"Now Millie, this last list will be what I want first, I am going to build a big shed to store material in," Jonas said.

"I will explain that to paw when I give it to him," she said.

"That will be good," Jonas answered.

Millie I was wondering, what is that growing out in that upper field?" Jonas asked.

You must be talking about the hemp, we have a market for it here in Kentucky, they use it to make ropes," she said.

"I have used rope made from it for a long time, but I never seen it growing before," Jonas replied.

"Well that's it," Millie said with a smile.

Jonas and Millie sat for a little while talking about Greenup County, and Kentucky. Jonas was curious about some of the things in this new place that he had come to.

"Millie how did the county get its name?" Jonas asked.

"They named it after Christopher Greenup is about all I know about that, I do know that he was a Governor one time," Millie answered.

"There seems to be several folks living about," Jonas said.

Crockett's Long Trip To Kentucky

"I heard Paw say we were getting up to about nine thousand in population," Millie said.

"That is a bunch of people," Jonas replied.

"Yes it is and we have several men from Kentucky serving in the war against Mexico," she said.

"Who is your Governor now?" Jonas asked.

"William Owsley is his name," she answered.

"I have heard of Henry Clay, he is a famous man from Kentucky isn't he?" Jonas asked.

"Yes he is, we just heard that his son Henry Clay Jr. was killed in the Mexican War, which saddened our whole state," Millie said.

"Sorry about that, it seems that the soldiers pay the price for the rich men's wars," Jonas added.

"Sad but true," Millie answered.

"Well Millie I see Crockett and Bill standing out there, guess I better go out and find them something to do," Jonas said.

"Jonas, Sunday is coming up, would you and Crockett like to go to church with us?" Millie asked.

"Do you all go to the little Baptist Church, we passed coming in the other day?" Jonas asked.

"Why yes, that is it," she answered.

"We will be glad to go and give it a try," Jonas said.

"What time do you leave?" Jonas asked.

"About 9:30, and you all can ride in our surrey, we have three seats so there will be room," she added.

Crockett's Long Trip To Kentucky

"Make sure it is alright with Samuel and let me know by Saturday," Jonas said.

"It will be fine, Paw already said," replied the smiling Millie.

"Alright then we will be ready, got to go, and thanks Millie," Jonas said with a smile.

Jonas got up and stepped off the porch and almost fell down looking back at Millie. Millie let out a little giggle.

Jonas grinned and headed back to the field where Crockett and Bill were waiting.

A few short days passed and it was Sunday morning. Jonas and Crockett cleaned up and put on their best duds. Jonas even shaved his whiskers and gave Crockett and himself a haircut.

About 9:25, the Truitt surrey pulled up to the front of the Truitt Inn.

"Paw you want me to go up and fetch Jonas?" Millie asked.

"Wait just a minute, it isn't 9:30 yet," Samuel said.

Millie was anxious to see Jonas and had become quite interested in the mill builder from Virginia.

"What time is it now Paw?" Millie asked again.

"Go ahead Millie, round them up," Samuel said.

About that time Jonas and Crockett appeared in the door way on their way to the awaiting Surrey. Millie had just stepped down and looked up to see them coming.

A big smile appeared on Millie's face as it did on Jonas's face. She stood by the surrey and waited for Jonas to take her hand and help her up.

Mary Truitt grinned at Samuel, and Samuel gave her a wink. Jonas took a seat by Millie and Crockett had the third seat all to himself. Samuel gave her a wink. Jonas took a seat by Millie and Crockett had the third seat all to himself.

"Get up Betsy," Samuel commanded the horse and away they went.

Crockett's Long Trip To Kentucky

Jonas and Crockett enjoyed their first Lords Day in Greenup County. They had a good service and Jonas felt at home with the congregation. The Minister was an elderly man by the name of John Young.

Samuel gave her a wink. Jonas took a seat by Millie and Crockett had the third seat all to himself.

Samuel gave her a wink. Jonas took a seat by Millie and Crockett had the third seat all to himself.

"Get up Betsy," Samuel commanded the horse and away they went.

Jonas and Crockett enjoyed their first Lords Day in Greenup County. They had a good service and Jonas felt at home with the congregation. The Minister was an elderly man by the name of John Young.

Samuel gave her a wink. Jonas took a seat by Millie and Crockett had the third seat all to himself.

"Get up Betsy," Samuel commanded the horse and away they went.

Jonas and Crockett enjoyed their first Lords Day in Greenup County. They had a good service and Jonas felt at home with the congregation. The Minister was an elderly man by the name of John Young.

"How old is Elder Young?" Jonas asked Millie.

"I think they said he will be eighty three on his next birthday," Millie answered.

"He looks old, but I would have guessed about seventy-two," Jonas said.

"Yes he doesn't show his age," Millie said.

"Paw is all Baptist preachers names Young?" Crockett asked from the back seat of the surrey.

"No son," Jonas said laughing.

"I doubt this John Young knows our David Young back in Tazewell County," Jonas added.

Crockett's Long Trip To Kentucky

"It is just a coincidence that both the Baptist churches have Preachers by the name of Young," Jonas explained.

Samuel struck up a conversation about this and that. After talking about Elder John Young and the church services, the topic went to the mill. Samuel could not help but think of the mill.

"Jonas I don't talk business on Sunday, but I wanted to let you know my brother George from Lewis County will arrive tomorrow sometime with six of his servants," Samuel said.

"After you get them started digging, you can head down to Carter County and see your brother to order your hardware," he added.

"Thank you sir, I will see to it," Jonas answered.

"Jonas, if you would like, come by the house and I will give you your material book back," Millie said.

"I will be by about 6:00 when it is nice and cool, and you can show me around a little more," Jonas said.

"That will be fine," Millie said with a smile.

Jonas and Crockett got out at the Inn and Samuel drove on to the house. Mary and Millie got out and Samuel took the Surrey to the big barn.

"Millie, you be real careful, Jonas is much older than you, I don't want you to get your heart broken," Mary said with concern.

"Don't worry Maw, I will be careful, Jonas is so smart and handsome," Millie answered.

Crockett and Jonas took off their best clothes and Crockett shed his shoes. They went down for dinner at the eatery.

Crockett's Long Trip To Kentucky

Louisa was busy with the Sunday meal. A large group always showed up on Sunday after church for dinner. Louisa had a big pile of chicken fried up, mashed potatoes, green beans from last year's crop, gravy and biscuits.

She was one busy little woman, going from table to table. Jonas and Crockett's favorite table by the window was taken so they found another one back in the corner.

"Paw do you think Millie is after you?" Crockett asked abruptly.

"I doubt that she is serious about me, would it be a bad thing, if she was?" Jonas asked.

"Well I reckon not, Maw has been gone a long time, I think it would be fine," Crockett said smiling.

"I may spend some time with her, will you get jealous?" Jonas asked.

"I want get jealous, Paw," Crockett answered sternly.

"Well I am glad to have your blessing, if we were to get serious, which I doubt," Jonas said.

After dinner Jonas and Crockett walked up into the woods and rested. They read the Bible, and talked much like they did on the Lords Day talked about the folks back home and about their new temporary home here in Kentucky.

They had a really good visit with each other; while enjoying the nice May weather. Jonas told Crockett about the trip he was going to take tomorrow to Carter County.

"What do you think Crockett, do you want to go with me or are you tired of traveling?" Jonas asked.

"Well what would I do if I stayed here?" Crockett asked.

"Fish, play, watch the men dig the trace, explore the surrounding hills and even wade the creek," Jonas said.

Crockett's Long Trip To Kentucky

"You are almost a man, and I think you are perfectly able to take care of yourself," Jonas added.

"You can go with me but you will have to ride one of the mules, what do you think?" Jonas asked.

"How long will you be gone?" Crockett asked.

"Four or five days I would think, two days or better traveling, and two days there with brother Richard's family," Jonas answered.

"Paw I think I will go, I haven't seen Uncle Richard for a year," Crockett said.

I haven't seen the cousins forever, and I wonder what James G. Whitt looks like, Crockett added.

"Paw, how come all your brother's name their children the same names, like Richard, Bunyon, and even James?" Crockett asked.

"I guess we just like some good old family names," Jonas answered.

"You know my cousins Richard Price Whitt and Abijah Whitt live in Carter County too," Jonas said.

"Richard P. has a son David Crockett Whitt born about two years after you," Jonas added.

"Reckon we might see him too paw?" Crockett asked.

"We will try to if it doesn't interfere with my business, I would love to see them all," Jonas added.

Jonas looked at his watch and it was almost supper time again.

"Paw it seems like we eat a lot, don't it?" Crockett asked.

"We are just on a schedule," Jonas answered.

Crockett's Long Trip To Kentucky

Jonas reminded Crockett that he and Millie were going to take a walk after supper.

"You can come with us or you can just play," Jonas informed him.

They went to have their supper, and the Truitt's sat at their regular table near them.

After supper and the normal conversations Jonas and Millie strolled out to walk up the creek. Jonas took Millie by the mill works and gave her a basic idea of the new mill's ongoing construction.

He explained that her Uncle George was coming ongoing construction. He explained that her Uncle George was coming tomorrow.

He would be bringing servants to start digging the trace. He also told her that Crockett and he were going to Carter County to see Richard the next day or the next.

"How long will you be gone?" Millie asked in a concerned voice.

"About four or five days I reckon," Jonas answered.

"Do you have to go now, Oh? I'm sorry for meddling in your business," She said.

"That is alright, I do have to go and get Richard started working on making the hardware for the mill, he is also my family, and we have not had a visit for some time," Jonas answered.

"Richard has a son named James G. Whitt, and my Crockett wants to meet him," Jonas said smiling.

Millie took Jonas by the hand and said, "Please hurry back then."

There was a fire of love beginning to burn between Jonas and Millie!

What does this lovely young lady see in me? Jonas thought. Well any way, I can't seem to hold back, what will be will be he thought.

Crockett's Long Trip To Kentucky

"Millie, I will be back in about five days, this will give us time to think where we are going with this relationship," Jonas said.

"I already know what I think, but five days separation will let you know," Millie said as she squeezed his hand.

Jonas felt the electric impulses of love flow from this beautiful creature.

Next morning brought a nice day, and it looked to get quite warm. They had a hot spell hit in the last week of May 1847 on Big White Oak.

Jonas and Crockett packed up a few things that they would need for the trip to Carter County and left it in their room. They had breakfast and walked around the marked of area for the dig.

George Truitt and Samuel came out of the house, and from around back of the big house came six big strong looking black men.

They were not guarded and looked to be healthy and wore rough but good clothes. They came in single file as if marching.

"Good morning Jonas, this is my brother George, he is going to get our digging took care of," Samuel said.

"Good morning George, good to meet you sir, and this is my son Crockett," Jonas said.

"Good to meet you Jonas and you too, Crockett," George said.

"These are my servants, and they love to work, Basel is the lead man, if you explain what you want done he will see to it," George said.

Jonas went over to Basel and stuck out his hand. Basel looked dumbfounded.

"Jonas you don't shake their hands that confuses them" George explained.

Jonas looked at George and back at Basel.

"Well Basel walk with me and I will show you the work," Jonas said.

Crockett's Long Trip To Kentucky

Jonas walked to the squared off part where they had already laid out, followed by Basel, George, and Samuel. The other five Negroes waited back where they had originally stopped.

Jonas showed Basel the eight feet by eight feet square staked out and string stretched around it, and then pointed down the creek at the staked out trace.

"Basel, I want you to dig a hole the size of the marked off area first, dig it down to bed rock, then start digging the marked area all the way to the creek, understand?" Jonas asked.

"Yep Sir Mister Jonas, I understand," Basel answered.

George smiled at Jonas!

"See Jonas he is a fine lead man and he will get the others going in short order," George said.

Basel went back to the other five and told them to go and get the picks and shovels and come back up to Jonas.

"Mister Jonas sir, you want the dirt put over toward the creek side sir?" asked Basel.

"That is right and I forgot to tell you, carry all the rocks back over there and pile them up as you dig them out," Jonas instructed as he pointed to a spot away from where the mill would be built.

Jonas looked at Crockett and saw an expression of amazement on the boy's face.

Jonas, Samuel, and George, walked back about ten paces to give the Negroes room to work.

"Jonas I will see Alfred Thompson today, and will get him started on the lumber order, Also I will leave Bill here with the workers," Samuel said.

"If you have any more instructions you can tell them to Bill and Basel, before you head out," Samuel added.

Crockett's Long Trip To Kentucky

"Alright Sir, I should be back about Friday or Saturday, Lord willing," Jonas said.

"Sir would you mind if Crockett rode that little filly with the blaze on her face?" Jonas asked.

"Not at all, I was going to offer her for the trip, but forgot," answered Samuel.

"Thank you sir, we better get a going," Jonas answered.

"Is Bill down at the barn?" Jonas asked.

"Think so Jonas and you might ought to go by the house and tell Millie good bye," Samuel said with a sneaky little grin on his face.

Jonas blushed a little and then headed toward the barn.

"Crockett will you go by and fetch our stuff we packed up, and also ask Louisa for a poke of vittles for the road," Jonas said.

"Sure will paw," Crockett answered.

"I am going to the barn and talk with Bill and get our mounts ready for the trip," Jonas said as he walked away.

Crockett hurried to the Inn to get their things and some food to take on the trip.

As he went he was thinking about the big black Negroes, and also about getting to ride Mister Truitt's little filly.

When Crockett got back to the barn, Jonas and Bill had the horses Jake, and Betsy saddled up.

Jonas looked in the packed items and dug out his old revolver and strapped it on.

"Expecting trouble Paw?" Crockett asked.

"No son, just want to be ready in case," Jonas answered.

Crockett's Long Trip To Kentucky

Then they tied on their satchels including the food Louisa gave Crockett. They mounted up, as Jonas was still talking to Bill. Then Bill looked at Crockett.

"Crockett, your mount is called Betsy, she is a sweet little gal to ride," Bill said.

"Thanks Bill, I will take extra good care of her," Crockett answered.

"Well son I am going to ride by the house and tell Millie good bye, you can ride with me and we will be off," Jonas said.

"Be right behind you Paw, get up Betsy," Crockett said.

Millie was waiting on the porch when Jonas and Crockett rode up. Jonas rode up close to the banister where Millie was holding on to.

"We are about to head south, so we come by to bid you farewell," Jonas said in a low voice.

"You all be real careful and hurry back," Millie said while she stuck out her hand.

Jonas reached and took her hand and gave it a gentle squeeze. They looked into each other's eyes as they felt the passion.

Jonas wheeled his horse and said in a much louder voice, "Farewell, we will see you in about five days."

"Good by Crockett, take care of your Paw and hurry back," Millie said.

"I will, and good by Miss Millie," Crockett answered.

Jonas led the way back by the mill construction to see if there were any more questions about the work. Bill was there and walked up to Jonas.

"Basel and his workers are getting right after it Jonas, they are down about a foot and a half already," Bill exclaimed.

Crockett's Long Trip To Kentucky

"If they get the trace dug all the way to the creek on the down creek end before I get back let them dig up the creek, but stop them about ten feet from the creek," Jonas instructed.

"We don't want the creek running though the trace while we build the mill," Jonas added.

"I understand completely," Bill answered.

"Got to go, we are burning day light," Jonas said.

"Be careful, see you all when you get back," Bill said.

Jonas and Crockett were trotting by the Inn by now, Samuel and Louisa came out and gave them a wave.

Jonas and Crockett waved their hands and were soon out of sight heading toward the Tygart Creek.

"We will keep a good pace, but watch not to over work our horses," Jonas said.

"Jake has not been ridden on a trip in a long time, and I don't know what shape Betsy is in," Jonas said in a concerned voice.

"Betsy seems to be up for it Paw," Crockett said.

"They are probably up for it more than our hind ends are," Jonas said with a little laugh.

It seemed like no time at all they were on the Tygart valley road heading south.

"Paw, where do we cross over to the Little Sandy River?" Crockett asked.

"Not sure, Sam said we couldn't miss the road across to the Little Sandy Valley," Jonas answered. (The road is now (Route 784)

"There is a little village near the other end of that road called Hopewell," Jonas added.

Crockett's Long Trip To Kentucky

"That is a good name, ain't it Paw?" Crockett asked.

"Ye-al it sounds good, could be named after someone named Hope," Jonas said.

The ride was going good but the heat of early June was starting to heat up the horses.

"The horses are doing fine for now, but we may have to go a little slower this afternoon," Jonas said.

"Paw maybe we can give them water and a little rest in Hopewell," Crockett said.

"Yes, but we can't tarry there for long, we have to get to Richard's before dark," Jonas emphasized.

As they rode along, they talked about first one thing then another. Crockett had some comments about the big black servants digging the trace.

"Paw ain't the Negroes "slaves," and don't they belong to Mister George Truitt?" Crockett asked.

"Well I reckon you are right son, servant is a word they use up this far north," Jonas said.

"The North criticizes the South about owning slaves, yet many of them have their own," Jonas said.

"We will have to watch what we say until we see how they talk about such matters," Jonas said.

"Paw I hope we get to stop by your first cousin's (Richard Price Whitt) so I can meet the younger David Crockett Whitt," Crockett said.

"We will certainly try too, Uncle Edmund lives thereabouts too, if he is still living, he is your Grand Paws brother," Jonas explained.

"That would be great if we got to see him Paw," Crockett announced.

Crockett's Long Trip To Kentucky

"Yes it would, but I am afraid he may have passed on by now," Jonas said.

"Paw, we have a lot of kin folks here in Kentucky, don't we?" Asked Crockett?

"We sure do, and down in Morgan County we have a lot of cousins that I don't even know," Jonas added.

Before they knew it they had crossed over into the Little Sandy valley; Then they moved south through the little town of Hopewell.

"I think we are making splendid time Crockett, let's stop and rest by the river under the shade of these beautiful trees, and give the horses a rest," Jonas said.

"I think we are all ready, especially my hind end," Crockett answered.

"Mine too," Jonas said with a little laugh.

They got the "vittles bag" and pulled out some fried chicken and biscuits; Then they had a nice little trail meal. They also watered Jake and Betsy, and then let them graze on some nice shade grass. They ate and rested for about a half an hour.

"We better get mounted up and get on up the river son," Jonas said.

"Paw, Betsy is keeping up with Jake just fine, I would love to have her for my own," Crockett said.

"That may be out of the question, Samuel has not mentioned letting her go," Jonas said.

"I know Paw, I was just wishing out loud," Crockett answered.

"Paw the Little Sandy River ain't that big is she?" Crockett asked.

"No not much bigger than Tygart," Jonas answered.

"Well how come Tygart is a creek and Little Sandy is a River?" Crockett asked.

Crockett's Long Trip To Kentucky

"A river is a river because of its length, not by how deep or wide it may be," Jonas explained.

"Does Little Sandy run a long way Paw?" Crockett asked.

"I have heard it runs deep into Kentucky, but don't really know," Jonas explained.

It was getting late in the afternoon, and Jonas began looking for the town of Grayson. They had passed the Carter County line away back, and even Jonas was getting anxious to reach his Brother Richard's property.

In a short time they came up on a little burg, and were told there was a Pig Iron Furnace just west of there. There were signs of much traffic, and there was also the smell of wood smoke in the air. They happened up on two men riding a wagon filled with gray looking dirt.

"Hello gentlemen," Jonas spoke as Crockett and he came along side of the wagon.

"Hello to you," said the driver of the wagon.

"What are you fellers hauling?" Jonas asked as he looked at the material in the wagon.

"Ore, that be Iron Ore," the driver answered.

"We be a taking it up here to Pactolus Furnace fer mister McMurty and Mister Ward," he added.

"I never seen it before," Jonas said.

"Wells, just where you fellers come from?" The driver asked.

"We are from Tazewell County Virginia, but are building a grist mill up in Greenup County, I am Jonas Whitt and this is my son Crockett," Jonas answered.

"What is Pac-to-lus?" Jonas asked.

Crockett's Long Trip To Kentucky

"Jonas I am Peter Johnson, this is Fred Reed, and Pactolus is just a place where there's a furnace," Peter said.

"Whitt, you say Whitt, Jonas?" Peter asked.

"Yes that is right, do you know any Whitt's here abouts?" Jonas asked.

I know Richard Whitt, he lives just about four or five miles south of Grayson," Peter answered.

"How far to is it to Grayson?" Jonas asked.

"Bout a mile or two," Fred spoke up.

"Would love to talk, but we need to get on up the river," Jonas said.

"We better get going too, Pactolus is a waiting," Peter said.

"Yeal, they need this Ore," Fred said.

"Nice meeting you all," Jonas said.

"You to Jonas, and you to Crockett," Peter said.

"Is Grayson very big Paw?" Crockett asked.

"Well son I have not seen it before, but I think it may be bout like all the other little county seats," Jonas answered.

"Paw we ain't passed many folks today, must not be too many lives round here except at Pactolus," Crockett exclaimed.

"I thought we would see more, myself," Jonas answered.

In about fifteen minutes they could see little spirals of smoke rising into the heavens, and the outline of some buildings.

"Well Crockett, I think that must be Grayson up ahead," Jonas announced.

"Must be, and I see a wagon heading this way Paw," Crockett said.

Crockett's Long Trip To Kentucky

"Most likely another ore wagon," Jonas surmised.

Jonas put Jake into a little faster gait, as they came closer to Grayson. Crockett lagged behind for about a minute and Betsy caught up with Jake.

Jonas pulled up Jake as he came up on the stopping wagon. This wagon was loaded with fire wood.

The man looked familiar to Jonas, even though the years makes changes to a man's appearance. Could this be some one that Jonas would know?

Both men looked at each other intently, as they greeted each other.

"Hello, Jonas Whitt is my name," Jonas said.

My goodness Jonas, I'm your cousin Abijah, Edmunds son," he said.

"I thought I knew you Abijah, how on earth are you?" Jonas answered.

"Me and Nancy are just fine, and all the kids are growing up," Abijah answered.

"What are you doing up here in Kentucky, Jonas?" Abijah asked.

"I have come to build a mill for Sam Truitt up in Greenup County, and I am heading down to visit brother Richard," Jonas answered.

"Who is that feller with you Jonas?" Abijah asked.

"This is my son David Crockett Whitt, he has come to help me with the mill building," Jonas said.

"Well hello cousin David, I guess we are second cousins, glad to meet you," Abijah said.

"Hello to you Cousin Abijah, glad to meet you," Crockett said in a bold manly voice.

"Where do you live?" Jonas asked.

Crockett's Long Trip To Kentucky

"Bout five miles on through Grayson, right on the Little Sandy, Me and Brother Richard bought a farm from Paw a few years back," Abijah answered.

"How is Uncle Edmund?" Jonas asked.

"Jonas he passed back in 1840'" Abijah answered.

"How about your Paw, is Hezekiah still living?" Abijah asked.

"No he and Maw both passed last year, and my bride Susannah passed back in thirty nine." Jonas exclaimed.

"Sorry to hear that Jonas, but we all got to go sometime I reckon," Abijah said.

"Yes but that don't make it easy does it?" Jonas asked.

"For sure, you be right on that," Abijah answered.

"Listen Jonas I got to get this wood delivered and get back home, won't you and Crockett stay with us tonight?" Abijah asked.

"How far is it from your place on to Brother Richards place?" Jonas asked.

"He lives on Big Gimlet Creek, about eight miles I reckon'" Abijah said.

"We will stop and see Cousin Richard Price Whitt. Then we will decide whether to go on today or not," Jonas said.

"Richard P. will be surprised to see you and Crockett, You know he has a David Crockett too, don't you?" asked Abijah.

"Yes, my Crockett wants to meet him," Jonas said.

"He ain't big as you Crockett," Abijah said.

"Well cousin go ahead and get your load delivered, and I will see you either tonight or on the way back from my brothers," Jonas exclaimed.

"Good, I look forward to it," Abijah exclaimed.

Crockett's Long Trip To Kentucky

"Get up Bill," Abijah commanded.

Abijah traveled toward Pactolus, Jonas and Crockett headed on to Grayson.

Jonas and Crockett slowed to have a look see, as they traveled through the town of Grayson. Then they picked up the pace to get on to the Abijah, Richard Price Whitt farm

"Nice town, ain't it Paw?" Crockett asked.

"Seems to be, I love this wide valley, and they have it on this rise for floods I bet" Jonas answered.

"We may stop in and look around a little on the way back if we have time," Jonas continued.

"Paw it won't make me and Betsy mad if we stay all night with our cousins," Crockett announced.

"I know what you mean, we might just do that," Jonas answered.

The mounts were still in good condition, so Jonas set a good pace of about eight miles per hour. Before they knew it they were almost to the Abijah, Richard Price Whitt Farm.

"I bet that next farm is it," Jonas announced.

"We made good time from Grayson, didn't we paw?" Crockett asked.

"Sure did, now let's just walk our horses the last quarter-mile so they can cool down," Jonas suggested.

"That will be good for them, won't it paw?" Crockett asked.

"Never put a horse away wet, they can die from such treatment, and never let them drink too much when they are still hot," Jonas instructed.

"I already knew that Paw, but it don't hurt none to be reminded," Crockett answered.

Crockett's Long Trip To Kentucky

Jonas and Crockett rode right up to the front porch, and a shotgun barrel comes out the door.

"Hold it right there," a woman's voice rang out.

"Don't shoot us Sarah, Jonas said in a loud voice.

"Who are you and what do you want?" Sarah asked.

"I'm your cousin Jonas Whitt, and my son Crockett is with me," Jonas answered.

The door opened and Sarah came out with a boy of about eight following. Jonas sat back and grinned at Sarah.

"Jonas Whitt, what in thunder are you doing way out here?" Sarah asked.

"We come to see my Cousins, Jonas said," with a big smile on his face.

"We passed Abijah bout an hour back, but where is Richard P.?" Jonas asked.

"He and the bigger children are out in the field, it is time for them to come in anyway." Sarah said, "I will ring the dinner bell, that will get them in here purty quick," She said.

"Who is this young man with you?" Sarah asked.

"This is my son David Crockett Whitt, and who might that be?" Jonas Asked.

"David Crockett, why that's my name," said the boy standing beside his mother.

"David Crockett Whitt meet your cousin David Crockett Whitt." Jonas announced.

Jonas's Crockett smiled and walked up to the smaller Crockett and stuck out his hand. The Younger one took his hand and shook it.

"Call me Crockett," said Jonas' son.

"Call me David," said Richard Price Whitt's son. Richard P. and the other children were in from the field and greatly surprised to see Jonas and Crockett. Every one hugged and told their names

Crockett's Long Trip To Kentucky

"I better get a going on dinner, Ann how bout washing you paws and give me some help getting these Whitt's something to eat," Sarah said.

"Paws," that is what Grand maw Rachel always said, ain't it Paw?" asked Crockett. "My Maw always says it too," said the younger David Crockett.

Jonas and Richard P. sat down in the shade of a big popular in his front yard.

"Jonas how have you been, is your Paw and Maw still living?" asked Richard P.

"Lost them both last year and lost my Bride Susannah, when little Hannah was born back in thirty nine," Jonas said.

"I talked to Abijah on the road just north of Grayson, he told me about the passing of Uncle Edmund," Jonas continued.

"We both had good parents, didn't we Jonas?" Asked Richard P?

"Sure did," Jonas said nodding.

"Did you move to the Blue Grass State, or are you just looking it over?" asked Richard P.

"My brother Richard got me hooked up with Samuel Truitt to build a grist mill," Jonas exclaimed. "How has Richard been, do you see him much?" asked Jonas.

"Devil Dick Richard, is doing just fine, he is still the big trickster he has always been," replied Richard P.

"Do they still call him that here in Kentucky?" Jonas asked.

Jonas and Richard P. sat down in the shade of a big Poplar in the front yard

"I talked to Abijah on the road just north of Grayson, he told me about the passing of Uncle Edmund," Jonas continued.

"We both had good parents, didn't we Jonas?" Asked Richard P?

"Sure did," Jonas said nodding.

"Did you move to the Blue Grass State, or are you just looking it over?" asked Richard P.

"My brother Richard got me hooked up with Samuel Truitt to build a grist mill," Jonas exclaimed. "How has Richard been, do you see him much?" asked Jonas.

"Devil Dick Richard, is doing just fine, he is still the big trickster he has always been," replied Richard P.

"Do they still call him that here in Kentucky?" Jonas asked.

"He is one of the nicest fellers I know, but the name stuck," said Richard P.

"He loves a prank better than anyone I know, back fired on him a few times you know," Richard P. continued. "Yes of course, that is how he got that handle," Jonas replied "

Do they still call him that here in Kentucky?" Jonas asked.

"He is one of the nicest feller I know, but the name stuck," said Richard P.

"He loves a prank better than anyone I know, back fired on him a few times you know," Richard P. continued.

"Yes of course, that is how he got that handle," Jonas replied.

"He is one big man that I never want to cross, cause he don't mind fight-un," Richard P. answered.

"How is his blacksmithing going?" Jonas asked.

Crockett's Long Trip To Kentucky

"Excellent, every time I am there he has a pile of work to do," Richard P. answered.

"That is the business end of my trip to Carter County, I have a big list of hardware for Brother Richard to fabricate, I owe him for getting me the job, now he will get the hardware job," Jonas said.

"By the way Richard, how far is his shop from here?" Jonas asked.

"He lives on Big Gimlet Creek that feeds into the Little Sandy, (Now just south of Grayson Lake) so I would guess seven or eight miles," answered Richard P.

"You and Crockett are staying with us tonight, you are tired and I want to get caught up on the news from Virginia," Richard P. insisted.

"Wash your "paws" and come and get it," Sarah said from the door way.

By the time supper was over Abijah arrived at his house which was located about one hundred yards from Richard P. Whitt's house. The two brothers were partners.

They were joint owners of the big farm. Actually it was two farms made from the one larger one purchased from Edmond Whitt.

The family bowed, and A prayer of Thanksgiving was lifted by Richard Price Whitt. They enjoyed a simple but delicious meal.

"Jonas do you want anything else to eat?" Ann asked.

This opened the door for the Old Whitt Saying.

"I have had sufficient," Jonas said.

Richard P. joined in, playing a hard of hearing old man and ask the question, *"Been a fish-un?"*

"Had a plenty," Jonas continued.

"Caught twenty?" Richard P. asked.

Had enough?" Jonas answered again.

"And they were tough?" asked Richard P.

Everyone laughed, especially the smaller children since they had not heard the old Whitt Saying.

Think I heard brother Abijah roll in about the time we did the fishing thing," Richard said.

"Will he and his family come over here you think?" Jonas asked.

"After they eat they will be right here," Richard P. answered.

"Jonas you didn't say anything about getting married again," Sarah said.

"No I haven't, it just about killed me when I lost my Susannah," Jonas said.

"Well do you have any prospects?" Sarah asked.

"Well Maybe," Jonas said with a sparkle in his eye.

"Miss Millie likes me and Paw," Crockett injected.

Jonas gave him a quick look.

"Abijah, Nancy, and their children arrived from next door. Greetings and hugs commence again. The Whitts all enjoyed a good visit and talked for hours.

Next morning the June sun was already bringing on the heat. Jonas and Crockett slept longer than usual as did the Richard P. family. Sarah and Ann, had the smell of coffee permeating the house, and the cows were balling.

"Get up Crockett, and smell the coffee," Jonas said.

"What is wrong with the cows, Paw?" Crockett asked.

"They want to be milked and put out to pasture I reckon," Jonas answered.

Crockett's Long Trip To Kentucky

In a little while everyone was up and had on their everyday work clothes. Jonas and Crockett would travel the seven to eight miles to Big Gimlet Creek, and the rest would go about their work once again.

After a breakfast of gravy and biscuits, the good byes were said. Jonas thanked the cousins for everything, then they headed over to the Abijah House and bid them a farewell.

The horsemen were on the move up the Little Sandy toward the Richard Devil Dick Black Smith Shop.

"Paw we kinda slept in, didn't we?" Crockett asked.

"Sure did, we were tired I reckon, all the riding yesterday and the good visits we had bout wore us out," Jonas answered.

"Crockett look at the way the land is changing," the Little Sandy seems to be in a canyon, just look at those beautiful cliffs," Jonas exclaimed.

"Paw this would be a dandy place to get ambushed wouldn't it?" Crockett asked.

"Yes it would, but I don't expect anything like that, Kentucky is a little tamer out here I think," Jonas answered.

"Cousin Richard and Abijah didn't give us any warning did they Paw?" Crockett asked.

"No they didn't, just enjoy the beauty of nature, I got my pistol if trouble would come," Jonas said confidently.

"This road is traveled a lot, just look at the horse and wagon tracks," Jonas said as he pointed to the road.

"We have been traveling for about an hour, so we will be coming up on Big Gimlet Creek any time," Jonas said.

"How far up the creek does Uncle Richard live, Paw?" Crockett asked.

"A short distance from the mouth, I was told," Jonas answered.

Crockett's Long Trip To Kentucky

"Little Sandy is starting to be little now," Crockett pointed out.

"Here comes a wagon now Paw," Crockett said as he looked way ahead.

"Yelp, I see it, looks to be loaded heavy, it has four horses pulling it," Jonas said.

"Probably more iron ore, Paw," Crockett answered.

In a few minutes the riders and the wagon met, and Jonas waved his hand in a friendly jester. The driver was friendly.

He said he had come from the Whitt Blacksmith Shop. He had a big load of hardware headed for the Ohio River. Jonas informed him that they were heading for the shop.

"Bout how far is it?" Jonas asked.

"Bout a quarter of a mile to the mouth of Big Gimlet Creek, then up the creek another quarter I reckon," answered the teamster.

"Thanks Sir, better let you go, you have a pretty good trip ahead of you," Jonas said.

"Any kind of trouble up ahead?" the teamster asked.

"We didn't have any or see any, why do you ask?" Jonas asked.

"Ever now in then there could be a bad man or two on the road," he answered.

"Be careful, and we will too," Jonas said.

The wagon began to move down river, and the Whitt's trotted toward Gimlet.

"Here's the mouth of the creek, and we go up the road beside it, Jonas said.

"There is a farm cabin, reckon that is Richards place?" Crockett asked.

"Nope, too soon, we are not up the creek far enough yet," Jonas said.

Crockett's Long Trip To Kentucky

In another five or six minute they could smell the wood smoke coming from the Whitt Black Smith Shop

A big flat area stretched out before them with a house, barn and a big blacksmith shop. Two wagons and a couple of saddle horses were tied out front.

"Now this is more like I envisioned it to be," Jonas said.

"It is a big shop and farm, ain't it Paw?" Crockett asked.

"Sure is son, hope Richard will be able to fill our order for the mill," Jonas answer.

Chapter 9
Order Is In, Get Back To Millie.

Jonas rode Jake right up to the hitching rail. Crockett followed with Betsy, and they dismounted and walked together into the big shop.

Four or five gentleman was standing around talking. Jonas looked over to a big man hammering hot metal on a big anvil. It was Richard Devil Dick Whitt, Jonas' big brother. I mean Big Brother.

Richard looked up and saw Jonas and Crockett but did not recognize them because he was engrossed in his work.

"I will be with you in a minute Sir, you know the old saying, got to strike while the iron is hot," Richard exclaimed.

Jonas gave him a wave and turned to the other gentleman and joined in their conversation. Crockett just stood there taking in the huge blacksmith shop, and marveled at his big uncle hammering out something out of red hot iron.

A big husky boy about the same age of Crockett came in the door carrying a picture of water to Richard. This must be James G. Whitt the younger son of Richard, Jonas thought.
Richard nodded his head at the young man to sit the water down on a nearby work bench.

"Thanks James," Richard said with a strong voice.

Richard took a big long drink, and then he took a rag and wiped the sweat from his brow and looked around. He gave Jonas and Crockett an intense look.

"Little brother is that you?" Richard asked.

Jonas waved his hand at his big brother and said, "Yes big brother it is me, Jonas."

Richard ran over to Jonas and picked him up giving him a big bear hug.

Crockett's Long Trip To Kentucky

"Hey Richard take it easy you are gonna break me in two," Jonas pleaded.

"What are you doing here; did you get that job from the Truitt's to build a mill?" Richard asked.

"That is right and I owe it all to you, I brought you a big job to fabricate the hardware for it," Jonas exclaimed.

Richard looked around at his patrons while saying, "This is my brother Jonas and his son Crockett."

"They are here from Virginia and I am shutting down the shop for the day," Richard added.
"Hey what about my?" the men tried to say.

Richard waved his hand to hush the customers.

"Men, my brother is here, I will make everything you need, just let me have this time with my family," Richard said.

The men meandered out the door while Jonas and Richard talked.

James G. Whitt, Richard's son of about the same age as Crockett saw the men leaving and wonders what was going on.

James G. came in the door and saw his Paw and this man and boy being really friendly.

"James come over here and meet your Uncle Jonas and Cousin Crockett," Richard said.

Crockett met him first with his hand out to shake. James the bigger boy took his hand and gave it a good firm shake.

"Good to meet you James," Crockett said in a really friendly manner.

"Glad to meet you too cousin," James answered.

Crockett's Long Trip To Kentucky

Then James went over to Jonas to greet him.

After all this Richard pointed to the door saying, "Let's get out of this hot shop Jonas and get cooled down."
"Becca will be glad to see you fellers," Richard said.

Richard led them to the house to see Becca and all the children.

Edmund Ned Whitt and John B. Whitt the sons of Richard Devil Dick Whitt were not at home. They were out on the road gathering materials for the black smith shop. The girls and of course Becca were extremely glad to see the relatives from Tazewell County.

"Becca, I shut down the shop for the day, you girls need to be a fixing something special for our dinner," Richard said with a smile.

"Ned and John will be back dreckly," Richard exclaimed.
"I will be glad to see them," exclaimed Jonas.

"Crockett has been talking about meeting John," Jonas said.

"Ned ain't a big man but he is plenty smart Jonas and John is taking after me, he is big and burly," Richard explained.

"I didn't mean John ain't smart just that he is a big man," Richard said.

"I understand," Jonas said smiling.

Jonas and Crockett spent two glorious days with the Richard Whitt family. Jonas and Richard transcribed the list of hardware, and went over every detail. Jonas even had sketches with precise measurements on some of the more important pieces.

Jonas explained that he needed certain pieces first, so there would be two deliveries to Truittville. They went over and established an estimated price including material and shipment.

Crockett's Long Trip To Kentucky

Crockett spent all of his time with Ned, John, and James. James G. was his favorite because of his age. They were both born in 1836. James G. was the senior of the two because James was a month older, so they could relate to each other better. James G. was stocky build, but Crockett was more slender and a full inch taller than his cousin.

Jonas had Millie on his mind and had become much more enamored with her than he thought. He tried not to show it, but Crockett could see his Paw was different.

They got up extra early on Friday and made an early start on their trip back. They stopped for a brief visit with the cousins, the Richard Price and Abijah Whitt families.

They let Betsy and Jake have a drink and trotted them toward the county seat of Carter County. Grayson was already busy as they passed through. They did not stop, but walked the horses real slowly so they could take in the sights of the town.

With good luck and a steady ride they would be back in Truittville before dark.

Becca had made them a poke of eats for the trail so they took advantage of it about 1:00 PM when they stopped to water and rest their mounts.

Jonas told Crockett that they were making good time and would be back in Tygart Valley before long.

"Paw, wonder how Tygart Creek got its name?" Crockett asked.

Millie told me it was named for the frontiersman Michael Tygart that discovered this great place. His friend Simon Kenton tried to get him to go on down the Ohio to Limestone (now Maysville) with him and settle. But Michael loved his creek.

She said that Michael was a poor swimmer and had drowned in his creek as he was trying to cross and fell from his horse.

"That is so sad," Crockett answered.

Crockett's Long Trip To Kentucky

"Yes it is," Jonas said.

"Who is this Simon Kenton?" Crockett asked.

"He was a worthy woodsman and Indian fighter," Jonas answered.

"Like Grand paw Hezekiah?" Crockett asked.

"Well I guess so, but Paw was not as famous as this Simon Kenton," Jonas explained.

"When the Indians come to attack Boones borough, ol Simon saved Daniel Boone twice in one day," Jonas said.

It was told that when they were under siege, Simon would slip out at night passing through the Indians and hunt during the day. The next night he would slip back in with a full deer on his shoulders. He kept the little group of Kentuckians from starving or giving up to the Indians.

"He must have been a strong man and very sneaky to get by the Indians," Crockett said.

"I reckon you are right on both accounts," Jonas replied.

After a long day's ride the Whitt's got back to Truittville about 8:00 PM Friday the 18th on June.

They had walked the horses the last half mile or so to let them cool down.

"Crockett will you take the horses to the barn and see to their needs, I need to see Sam for a short meeting," Jonas said.

"I will meet you later at the Inn and have some supper," Jonas continued.
"That will be fine Paw, I will be ready to eat for sure," Crockett said in a tired voice.

Jonas took his book and headed to the Truitt House to see Sam and of course Millie.

Crockett's Long Trip To Kentucky

Crockett stopped by the Inn to let Louisa know that Jonas and he would need something to eat in about an hour. She told him that she would find something, and asked about their trip to Carter County. Crockett gave her a short version, so he could get the horses taken care of.

Jonas and Samuel talk briefly about the price and delivery of the hardware from Big Gimlet Creek. The hardware and delivery would cost Samuel Truitt one hundred dollars.

Sam said, "Fine," and did not bat an eye.

"I am glad that your brother Richard is doing it, it seems like a fair price in today's market," Samuel said.

"There is a lot of work there!" Jonas exclaimed.

"Alfred Thompson is bringing you the first order of lumber tomorrow," Samuel announced.

"Wonder if he has the storage shed material first?" Jonas asked.

"That is what he said and also some of the extra timbers for the mill," Samuel answered.

"I guess you saw that the men have dug down to rock bottom and almost to the creek on the downstream side?" Samuel asked.

"I didn't get a good look but I saw they have done a lot of work by the size of the piled up dirt," Jonas said.

Jonas saw Millie in the other room waiting to greet him.

"Sounds good Samuel, I will talk with you tomorrow and go over anything you might have questions about," Jonas said.

About that time Millie walked into the room and asks if they wanted anything to drink. Samuel took this as a sign to leave her and Jonas alone.

Crockett's Long Trip To Kentucky

"I will see you tomorrow Jonas," Samuel said as he left the room.

"Yes sir," Jonas answered.

Millie walked up close to Jonas and took his hand.

Jonas could not help himself; he put his arms around her.

"Sorry if I am smelling a bit gamey, been on the road all day," Jonas said.

"You smell perfect to me," she said as she pulled Jonas up against her full breast.

Jonas stole a little kiss and said he would see her tomorrow.

"I have to get over to the Inn with Crockett and eat a bite," Jonas exclaimed.

"I am just about tired out and very hungry," Jonas added.

"I understand Sweetheart, you go and eat," Millie said in her most sweet voice.

"We will talk tomorrow and spend some time together on Sunday," she said.

"I look forward to it sweet Millie," Jonas said.

Jonas left her and his heart was throbbing. He had not felt this way since Susannah and he experienced young love.

"I think my Susannah would want me to love again," Jonas thought.

Jonas arrives back at the Inn about the same time as Crockett.

"Did you get the horses cared for son?" Jonas asked.

"Sure did, how was your meeting with Mister Truitt?" Crockett asked.

"Went good and I also saw Millie," Jonas said.

Crockett's Long Trip To Kentucky

"Paw I really like that little filly, she was a good horse to ride," Crockett said.

Jonas laughed.

"What is it Paw?" Crockett asked.

"I was talking about Millie and you changed the subject in mid-stream about Betsy," Jonas said.

Crockett laughed.

"Miss Millie sure ain't no horse is she Paw?" Crockett asked.

"She sure ain't," Jonas agreed.

Louisa fried up some pork chops and added some left over soup beans and cornbread for Jonas and Crockett.

"We will sleep good tonight," Crockett said after enjoying the good meal.

"I reckon we will son," Jonas said with a grin.

Morning came in a hurry for Jonas and Crockett, because they were really tired. It was Saturday morning and a work day, even though Saturdays were treated a little different in public works. Jonas would probably have to unload a wagon or two of lumber.

Alfred Thompson was supposed to show up with the first shipment of lumber. Jonas didn't expect him before afternoon. Jonas would not work too hard today doing mostly planning and going over directions with Basel about the dig. Jonas would talk to Bill Thompson also about his future plans.

Crockett was a faithful little worker, and he knew most of the tools Jonas used in the mill work. Jonas was always patient with Crockett and showed him many things about building. Crockett enjoyed all aspects of building and that made him a good apprentice.

After a leisurely breakfast, Jonas and Crockett went out to the job site to look

Crockett's Long Trip To Kentucky

everything over. Jonas was impressed with the amount of earth the servants had dug out. Jonas was also impressed with the precise cut right up to the stretched line and stakes.

Basel had his men going at it and the dirt was flying. Also they had accumulated a great pile of large and small creek rocks. They had even separated them into two piles, one of larger and one for the small stones.

The stones would be laid up inside the pit where the under shot water wheel would be located so the precise measure of water could flow through. It would be like two walls with just enough space for the wheel to turn between them. There would also be a need for some foundation and chimney work. A few would be needed to be laid up at the mouth of the trace so that water could be blocked with heavy boards when the mill was shut down. The rest of the stones would be put in the creek just below the mouth of the trace to form a dam.

Jonas went up and greeted the Negroes and gave them a well done.

"Thank you Basel and the rest of you fellers for the good work," Jonas said.

"You welcome Mister Jonas, wee's tried our best to get her done, fore you and young Crockett gets back, but had some miseries with some of duh work," Basel explained.

"Don't worry about it, you fellers have done a splendid job so far, just keep up the good work and before long you will have it done," Jonas commended.

The day passed fast. Jonas, Bill and Crockett unloaded two loads of lumber right after dinner. Jonas was pleased overall with the progress. He told Bill Thompson and Crockett that they would lay out the shed first thing Monday morning.

"Jonas, what is the shed for?" Bill asked.

Crockett started to answer, but waited respectfully for Jonas to give an answer.

"We will store materials in it and also have a place to get out of the weather while we are building," Jonas explained.

Crockett's Long Trip To Kentucky

"When we have the mill up and running the shed can be used for any number of things," Jonas continued.

Supper time came, and neither Samuel nor Millie had come to talk. Jonas was glad not to be interrupted while he was working.

Finally George Truitt came out and told Basel to knock off for the day.

"Thank you Mister George, we bin getting her all dug out," Basel answered.

"That's fine Basel, you and the boys go out back and get ready for your supper," George told them.

The Negroes came up out of the trace, each carrying a pick or shovel and marched single file to a tent set up out behind the Truitt house.

George had a table for them to have their meals on. He also provided a cut off barrel full of water to wash off in. They slept in the big tent that they brought with them from Lewis County.

Crockett stood gawking at the site of the black men marching toward the back of the house.

"Come on Crockett, let's go and get ready for our supper too," Jonas said when he saw Crockett staring at the blacks.

"Paw, ain't Basel and the others slaves?" Crockett asked.

"Yes son, but they desire to call them servants this far north, so while we are here we will do the same," Jonas said in a quiet voice.

"I know; when in Rome do as the Romans do, uh paw?" Crockett asked.

"Crockett some folks up north are hypocrites about slavery, I am still feeling out the folks round here to see how they think about such matters," Jonas said.

"So you want me not to say anything about it, uh Paw?" Crockett asked.

Crockett's Long Trip To Kentucky

"That is right son, we have good work opportunities here in Greenup County and don't need any friction," Jonas explained.

The Truitt's came to the Inn for their supper and sat at their table close to Jonas and Crockett. After supper Jonas walked Millie back to the house and sat on the porch for a while.

As twilight came to Greenup County the lightning bugs began to decorate the hills with their little lights. Evening sounds of insects, frogs and birds gave a soothing feeling to all that could hear the music of nature.

Crockett and some of the other boys in the area chased after the fireflies and laughed as they played.

Sounds from behind the house began to fill the air as the slaves sang some of their hymns in a low even tempo. Crockett stopped to listen, he had never heard singing like this before. It had a ring of a foreign language, yet it was understandable. These black men had a rhythm and sound that Jonas and Crockett had never seen or heard. They were hymns of faith the listeners could readily discern.

Jonas and Millie could be heard in a whispering sound undistinguishable to others.

Crockett tired of the play and came up to the porch.

"What is it son," Jonas asked.

"I am tired Paw, will it be alright if I head back to the room?" Crockett asked.

"Sure son, I will be along dreckly, be sure to wash up before you get in your bed," Jonas said.

"I will paw," Crockett answered.

Jonas and Millie talked for a little while longer. Jonas told her that he missed his little daughter Hannah and is going to figure a way to get her to Kentucky.

"She is going to be grown up before I know it," Jonas said.

Crockett's Long Trip To Kentucky

"Get her here Jonas, she can stay with me in our house, that way we can get to know each other," Millie offered.

"Thank you so much, you are so sweet to offer my baby girl this opportunity, but what would your parents say?" Jonas asked.

"They would be proud to have a young girl come into their lives," she said.

"Trust me in this Jonas," Millie reiterated.

"I will write to my brother James tomorrow and see if he can find a way to get her here," Jonas said.

Jonas was elated with the idea of Hannah being here with him and Crockett.

It was almost dark and Jonas put his arm around Millie and pulled her close to him.

"Millie, I am much older than you, are you sure of your feelings about me?" Jonas asked.

"Can you not feel the love I have for you, Jonas Whitt?" she asked.

"I know what I feel, and hope you are having this same strong attraction I am experiencing for you," Jonas said.

"I am afraid I have fallen for you Mister Whitt," she said.

Jonas gave her an affectionate kiss and got up.

"Better go and get some sleep, a most attractive woman and her parents will be waiting outside for me tomorrow morning," Jonas said.

"Tomorrow is the Lords day isn't it?" Millie answered.

"Alright sweet heart, I will turn you lose for now," Millie said in a sweet voice.

Crockett's Long Trip To Kentucky

"Good night sweetheart, I will see you in the morning," Jonas said as he turned to leave.

"Good night Mister Whitt," Millie said in a much louder voice.

This was for the benefit of any ears that may be listening.

Crockett had already washed off and was in his bunk.

Jonas and Crockett talked while Jonas got ready for bed. Jonas told Crockett that he is writing a letter tomorrow to James in Virginia.

"I am going to have him work to help Hannah get to Kentucky," Jonas said. Millie said, "Hannah could stay over there with the Truitt's."

"What do you think son?" Jonas asked.

"It sounds real good to me, Paw," Crockett answered.

"Reckon Uncle James can get her to us somehow?" Crockett asked.

"We can sure try, can't we son?" Jonas asked.

After a good night and a restful Lords Day, it is Monday again. Jonas wrote a letter to James, Hannah, and the family explaining his desire to get Hannah to Kentucky. He explained that Hannah would be able to stay in the big Truitt house with his lady friend, Mildred Truitt. Jonas asked his brother James to go to work and find a way for Hannah to get to Kentucky.

Crockett was elated with the idea that somehow, someway Hannah could come to Truittville. Even though Hannah and Crockett did not see eye to eye on some things, they still loved each other.

Crockett had made friends with some boys in Kentucky, but they were not family. The boys were sons of other men that worked for Samuel Truitt. The shoe maker's son was little Tony Montivon. The farmhand's sons were also friends with Crockett. Billy Miller, and John Quillen were just a little older than Crockett but that didn't matter.

Crockett's Long Trip To Kentucky

Jonas always turned Crockett loose from work when the other boys came to play.

They explored the nearby hills, branches, and of course spent time in Big White Oak Creek.

Jonas, Bill Thompson and Crockett laid out the shed, and started digging holes for the timbers. It was a building somewhat like modern pole buildings. The plan came right from Jonas' mill building book. Jonas had been careful to write down all measurements and even drew sketches while building past mills and buildings.

The servants as Samuel called them were back in the trace still digging downstream. Their work was coming along good. They would start digging the trace back upstream just as soon as they cut into the creek on the downstream end.

Jonas made it a point to give Samuel his letter to James for mailing, and ask if Millie had talked to him about Hannah coming.

Samuel was for the plan. "Polly will be tickled to death to have a young girl in the house again, Mary Elizabeth was getting to be an adult." he exclaimed.

Crockett's Long Trip To Kentucky

Chapter 10
Hannah's Coming To Kentucky

Jonas and Crockett get an answer to their first letter. After the post rider came by the Truittville Post Office, Samuel brought the letter straight to Jonas. Jonas thanked Samuel for bringing the letter so quickly. Jonas opened the letter slow and deliberately with Crockett looking on.
"It is from Brother James," Jonas thought out loud.

Crockett moves in even closer, wanting to hear every word.

Jonas skims over the letter quickly without saying a word.

"Paw, what does it say?" asked Crockett impatiently.

"Alright son, hold on and I will read it to you," Jonas answered.

Here is what it says,
Greetings Jonas and Crockett.
We received your letter yesterday and are glad to hear of your safe arrival in Greenup, County. Things are fine here with the exception of Hannah wanting to come to you. I never thought she would miss you all so much.

Are you in any position to receive her there in Kentucky? We have tried everything to take her mind off of you and Crockett. James Griffith has expressed that he would bring her to you, and have a little visit, if practical.

Have you seen Brother Richard yet? He will be glad to see you and Crockett.

How is the mill coming along?

We are all doing fine. All your children and grandchildren are doing fine.

If at all possible, make arrangements to receive your Hannah, and I will send her to you by James Griffith.
Your big brother James.

Crockett's Long Trip To Kentucky

"Wow Paw, Hannah and James Griffith may be on their way here, since this is the answer to the first letter," Crockett said.

"Yes you are right, if they got our second letter," Jonas exclaimed.

I will send another letter tomorrow, just in case they didn't get our letter asking James to find a way to get her to us," Jonas said.

"Good idea Paw, but I bet James Griffith and Hannah are on the way," Crockett said excitedly.

The mill work was coming along good. The slaves have completed digging the fifty yard trace with exception of about ten feet on the upstream end. They were instructed to leave it that way until the mill work progressed. Jonas did not want to fight the water in the trace while constructing the mill.

The storage shed was up, and some of the stone work in the trace was finished. Jonas has been cutting out the boards to build the water wheel.

Crockett had been with his Paw most everyday helping get tools and in many other ways. Crockett took off now and then to play with his friends and take an occasional dip in the creek.

Signs of fall were already appearing faintly.

"It is good that we have our shed done, well before winter comes, there will be plenty of work we can do all winter long," Jonas affirmed.

John Bunyon and James G. Whitt arrived Wednesday August 25, 1847, with the first shipment of hardware from Gimlet Creek. Crockett was extremely glad to see his cousin James G. Whitt.

The work done by Richard Whitt was excellent and Samuel was pleased as well as Jonas.

Crockett and James G. had a good time playing and the other boys liked Crockett's Cousin from Carter County.

Crockett's Long Trip To Kentucky

John Bunyon, Jonas' nephew was impressed with the mill project, and the work creditability of his Uncle Jonas.

Jonas instructed John Bunyon to tell Richard that Samuel Truitt was pleased with his work as well as was he.

Samuel was pleased with the progress, and handed John Bunyon payment in gold for the first of two shipments.

Early next morning John Bunyon Whitt and James G. Whitt headed down stream toward their fathers shop in Carter County. Jonas and Crockett bid them farewell. Jonas said for them to bring Richard on the next shipment. They said they would try.

Samuel mentioned to Jonas that school would start in October.

Jonas informed Crockett, that Samuel Truitt would start school sometime in October.

"School!" you will need me to help with the mill, Paw," Crockett exclaimed.

"Mister Truitt is well educated Crockett, and you are fortunate to have such a man to teach you," Jonas said.

"He knows doctoring, engineering, running business, the three R's, and of course teaching," Jonas said.

"Have you seen his penmanship, Crockett?" Jonas asked.

"Yes Paw, Mister Truitt has a great hand writing," Crockett confessed.

"It will be sometime before school starts, so enjoy the season," Jonas said.

Jonas and Millie had become really close; they spent time together most every evening and also on the Lords Day. People began to speculate as to when an announcement may be forthcoming.

Crockett's Long Trip To Kentucky

Even Crockett's friends began to tease him about his Paw and Millie. This did not set well with Crockett and he felt a little resentment toward Millie Truitt.

Millie has done nothing but give Crockett her best. Millie and Jonas could not help it, they were in love. Jonas walked around all day with a smile on his face, as did Millie.

James Griffith and Hannah left Tazewell County August 20, 1847 on horseback. They would make the trip much faster than did Jonas and Crockett as they were not riding a heavy wagon. If they have a good trip they could be in Truittville by the first week of September.

Friday September the tenth, James Griffith and Hannah rode into Truittville about supper time.

Jonas and Crockett were walking toward the Truitt Inn, and Crockett said, "There is James and Hannah!"

Crockett took off in a run and Jonas followed.

"Well I be!" Jonas said excitedly.

Hannah leaped from her horse and ran to her Paw and brother Crockett. James Griffith Whitt got down from his horse elated to see the reunion. After hugging Hannah Jonas walked up to James Griffith and gave him a big hug.

"Thank you son for doing this for me and Hannah," Jonas said.

"Welcome Paw, I wanted to see how you and Crockett were fairing' too, I like Greenup County," James exclaimed as he scanned the beautiful little valley.

"I have been anxious to see Kentucky since you and Crockett left," James Griffith continued.

"Did you all have any trouble on the road?" Jonas asked.

"No sir, we talked to some folks that remember you and Crockett traveling through, "James Griffith said.

Crockett's Long Trip To Kentucky

"Dan McCoy and his wife Bertha both talked highly of you, they made us stay all night with them," James Griffith said.

"They said you showed them how to pray, Paw, you taught me too," Hannah exclaimed.

"You learned quickly my little darling," Jonas said with a smile.

"Well Paw, it is easy, Jesus is my friend and I just talk to him," she answered.

"That is a really good answer," Jonas said.

By now Samuel, Polly and Millie were there on their way to supper, and of course to meet Hannah and James Griffith.

"Let me get someone to take care of your ponies and you can visit as you eat supper," Samuel said.

"Thank you Sam, that would be real nice of you," Jonas answered.

Everyone greeted each other and went in the Inn. Samuel was back from the barn in short order.

"Got a boy caring for your horses, did I miss anything?" Samuel asked.

"Don't think so," Jonas answered.

Louisa became excited when she saw that Hannah and James Griffith Whitt had arrived. She took them all to the biggest table so they all could eat together and visit. Millie sat beside Jonas and he had Hannah and Crockett on his other side. Jonas kept hugging Hannah as they talked.

Louisa was a little taken by the handsome James Griffith Whitt. She kept leaning on him while she served up the supper. He turned once and gave her a special smile that she instantly returned. He enjoyed the attention of Louisa, especially when she leaned her full bosom on his shoulder.

Crockett's Long Trip To Kentucky

Crockett was really glad to see his little sister and big brother. They both were really glad to see Crockett also.

"Crockett, you must have grown a foot since you left Virginia," James said.

"It's this good Kentucky food Louisa is feeding him," Jonas commented.

Alfred Thompson the lumberman came into the dining room to get some supper, and Hannah noticed him.

"Who is that man?" she asked Jonas in a whisper.

"He is a lumberman that is bringing the lumber for the mill, why do you ask? Jonas asked.

"I think he is handsome," Hannah said.

"Honey you are just a baby," Jonas said.

"I will always be your baby, Paw!" she answered.

The Whitts and Truitts sat for hours visiting and getting acquainted. Each one having a time to tell a story or ask a question.

"James Griffith had to inquire about Crockett's letter home, "what was that about seeing naked women on your trip?"

Crockett turned a little pink.

Jonas saw Crockett was embarrassed so he came to his aid.

"We will tell you all about our trip when we have more time," Jonas said.

"It is getting late, we had better get ready for bed," Jonas continued.

"Hannah you come to our house to sleep in my room," Millie said.

"James Griffith, you can have a room here at the Inn, on me, Louisa will take care of you, and find you a good room," Samuel said.

Crockett and James Griffith followed Louisa up stairs to show them his room. Jonas walked arm and arm with Hannah and Millie back to the Truitt house.

Samuel and Polly said, "Good night all," and went into the house.

Jonas gave both of his favorite girls a hug. He looked into the beautiful hazel eyes of Hannah.

"You look so much like your Maw, long as you live Susannah lives in you," Jonas said.

Then he took Millie into his arms and gave her a little kiss.

"I will see you all tomorrow," Jonas said as he headed off the porch.

"By Paw," Hannah answered.

"Good night Mister Whitt," Millie said sweetly.

Millie and Hannah went into the house elated with the day's happenings of the two finally meeting.

"I am so glad that you are here Hannah," Millie said.

"Me too, are you and Paw fixing to get married?" Hannah asked abruptly.

"How would you feel about that?" Millie asked.

"Well if it makes Paw happy I am for it, I don't remember my Maw, cept by the stories I heard," Hannah said.

"Well honey, if you look like her as your Paw says she was very beautiful," Millie said.

"Everyone says she was a beautiful and wonderful lady," Hannah said.

Crockett's Long Trip To Kentucky

"Well to answer your question, your Paw has not come right out and asked me yet, but I hope he will," Millie said.

"Miss Millie, you are a beautiful lady too," Hannah said.

"Well thank you Hannah, I am glad you think so," said a surprised Millie.

"You know I or nobody else could take your Maws place, but I do love your Paw," said Millie.

"I understand Miss Millie," Hannah said.

Back in the Inn, James Griffith and Crockett talked away the hours.

Finally Jonas spoke up, "boys it's time to get some sleep, some folks have to work tomorrow."

"Sounds like old times don't it Crockett?" James asked.

"What's that brother?" Crockett asked.

"Paw telling us to go to sleep," James Griffith said laughing.
"Alright Paw we will hush up, I am going to my room," James said.

"Good night son," Jonas said as James was leaving the room.

"Good night Paw, and good night to you little brother," James said, closing the door.

Morning came quickly to those that had visited late into the night. All of the Whitt's were groggy and were ready for that first cup of coffee.

Word spread quickly around the little community of Truittville that James Griffith Whitt and the fine little lady Hannah Whitt had arrived last evening.
Little Tony, Billy Miller, and Johnny
Quillen were hanging out to get a glimpse of the new young lady from Virginia. Even the older people were curious to see James Griffith and Hannah.

Crockett's Long Trip To Kentucky

Jonas would do little work this day, he would get Bill Thompson started on some of the wood sawing and drilling. Also Alfred Thompson had arrived last evening with more lumber and timbers so that would have to be unloaded and stored in the big shed.

James, Griffith and Crockett would help with the unloading and whatever Jonas wanted them to do. Jonas told them to help with the lumber and then he would take time to visit some more.
Samuel saw James Griffith, Crockett, Jonas, Bill Thompson, and Alfred Thompson all working like beavers. He went over to Jonas and told him to take the afternoon off so he could spend some time with the family. Jonas told Samuel he had made a deal with his sons, that if they would help get rid of the wagon he would take off some time.

Millie and Hannah slept in a little late this morning, and leisurely walked over to the Inn for their breakfast.

Crockett's friends lined up and gawked at Hannah as she swayed by. She rolled her big hazel eyes at them but said nothing.

Millie smiled at the situation.

James Griffith was friendly and enjoyed the attention of Louisa Truitt, but he did nothing out of the way. He remembered his sweetheart Nancy Webb, back in Baptist Valley Virginia.

The Truitts and Whitts all gathered for supper a little early. An evening of visiting and telling stories would be the theme at the big table.

James Griffith Whitt stayed for two more days, and left for Virginia via Carter County. He decided to go by and visit his cousins and Uncle Richard on Gimlet Creek. Then he wanted to stop off and see his Uncle John Bunyon near Maytown, in Floyd County. He thought he may never have this chance again, since it was quite a trip through the mountains and consumed much time.

Everyone gathered around the morning James prepared to leave. He hugged all the Whitt's, Millie, and Louisa Truitt. He shook hands with all the rest of the folks, and personally thanked Samuel Truitt for the great hospitably. James Griffith got

Crockett's Long Trip To Kentucky

on his horse, took the bag of traveling food Louisa had prepared.

James Griffith Whitt reared up his saddle horse, waved, and turned down Big White Oak Creek, and did not look back. Everyone was sad to see him leave, especially Hannah, Crockett, and Louisa Truitt.

Time seemed to fly by. It was mid-October and Crockett and Hannah joined the other Truittville children in the church each day for school. Samuel Truitt was a masterful teacher that truly inspired the students, even though the boys grew tired of writing each letter repeatedly. Samuel wanted each child to express themselves in excellent penmanship. Samuel demanded that each student write each letter perfectly before he allowed them to go to the next. Finally the children began to see the fruits of the redundant writing of each letter.

Samuel also taught the children history and government of this new nation. He instilled the importance of voting and taking part of civic duties. He also taught them arithmetic, and even some general things like business. He read a Bible story each day.

Samuel taught the boys the basics of civil engineering, and farming. He had Millie come and teach the girls about sewing, quilting, and cooking while he worked with the boys.

Crockett liked school for the first time. There was a good looking older girl in his class that he adored. Millie's little sister Mary Elizabeth Truitt was about four years older than Crockett, but that did not hold back the attraction shared by the two.

The mill work progressed a little each day. The great twenty foot water wheel was finished and stood menacing on the foundation and shaft. It stood there in a waterless trace waiting for a job to do.

Some of the other foundation was laid out and waiting for scheduled materials to arrive. Each part of the mill had to be built in the proper sequence, to insure proper operation and future maintenance.

Jonas always told Crockett, "Some things just can't be rushed."

Crockett's Long Trip To Kentucky

"It's kinda like a big clock, ain't it Paw?" Crockett asked.

"That is a real good analysis," Jonas answered.

"Paw you know a lot of big words, don't you?" Crockett asked.

"I sure do, I know Mississippi and watermelon," Jonas said laughingly.

Crockett laughed too!"

Jonas and Millie were spending even more time together. A wedding date was expected to be announced anytime.

Jonas went to Samuel and Polly Truitt late in the evening on November 21, 1847.
    "Sir I need to speak to you and Miss Polly, if this is a convenient time?" Jonas asked.

"We can talk now, is something going amiss with the mill?" Samuel asked.

"Let the man talk Sam, Jonas has something important to ask us," Polly inserted.

"Oh," Samuel answered with a special interest.

"Sir, and Miss Polly, you know that Millie and I have been keeping company purty steady as late," Jonas said.

"Well yes Jonas, go ahead and tell us what's on your mind," Samuel said.

"Shhh! let him talk Sam," Polly countered.

"I have asked Miss Millie to marry me providing you give us permission," Jonas said.
"If that is a question Jonas, we give our blessing, don't we Polly?" Samuel asked.

"I was concerned about our age difference, but Millie said that don't count for nothing sir," Jonas said.

"Polly and I have talked many times of this moment Jonas, and have come up with

Crockett's Long Trip To Kentucky

the same answer," Samuel said.

"Sir I promise to love her and take the best of care of her," Jonas said.

Finally Polly got to speak again.

"Jonas I think you and Millie will make a great couple, but will you wait another two or three months to make sure?" Polly asked, surprising them both.

"I think that is a fair request Ma-um," Jonas answered.

"If Millie agrees we can wait until early spring," Jonas continued.

"Be alright if I talk to her and tell her what we have decided?" Jonas asked.

"I will go and fetch her, she is upstairs teaching Hannah cross-stitch," Polly said.

Chapter 11
Jonas Takes A bride

Jonas is waiting with Samuel as Hannah and Millie descend the stairs. Samuel has a glass of wine in his hand, and held it high when Millie came in the room.

"Well Paw, what are you doing?" Millie asked.

Jonas was standing there awkwardly waiting to talk to his lady friend.

"Plans are being made and Jonas wants to talk to you about it," Samuel said.

"What is it Paw?" Hannah asked in anticipation.

Finally Jonas got to speak. He looked around at everyone and then straight into the eyes of Millie Truitt.

"Millie if you will agree, we can be married in two or three months," Jonas said.

"I agree," Millie said excitedly.

"But why wait two or three months?" she asked, as she looked at Samuel and Polly.

"We all just want you to be really sure," Jonas said.

"Paw and Millie's getting married!" Hannah shouted gleefully.

Crockett is over at the Inn wondering what his Paw is doing this evening. He has felt neglected by Jonas and even Hannah lately. He has enjoyed school with Samuel Truitt being his school master, and the lovely Mary Elizabeth Truitt being in the class.

The November evening was cold so Crockett put another chunk of wood in the little iron stove. Where is Paw, he thought? He is most likely with that woman, I am afraid he might get married, then what will happen to me, Crockett continued in thought. I may have to just up and leave, he thought. Uncle James and Nancy would be glad to have me, he thought. I could even stay with James Griffith on the Indian Creek farm, he considered.

His thoughts were interrupted with a knock on the door.

Crockett opened the door, "It's just me Jonas," Jonas said.

Crockett's Long Trip To Kentucky

Crockett was back from his world of thoughts.

"Come in Paw it's cold out tonight," Crockett answered.

As Jonas comes in out of the cold hallway he has a big smile on his face.

"What you been doing son?" Jonas asked.

"I studied from this book a little bit, and kept the fire," Crockett answered.

"What book is it?" Jonas asked.

"It's about the war here in Kentucky Paw," Crockett said.

"What war?" Jonas asked.

"You know Paw, about the Indians and British fighting the people at Boonsboro," Crockett answered.

"Our forefathers paid a price so we could have this free country didn't they son?" Jonas asked.

"Sure did, I would have loved to meet that Simon Kenton and Daniel Boone, wouldn't you paw?" Crockett asked.

"Fine men, son," Jonas answered.

"I have something to tell you Crockett," Jonas said.

Here it comes, thought Crockett.

"Well what is it Paw?" Crockett asked.

"I have been over to the Truitts and have asked Millie to marry me," Jonas said.

Crockett's countenance fell!

"What's wrong son?" Jonas asked as he seen the visible difference in his son.

"Why do you have to marry her Paw? Why?" Crockett asked in a raised voice.

Jonas was greatly surprised, at his son!

"What will happen to me?" Crockett asked.

"You will be just fine son, you will live with me, Millie and Hannah," Jonas explained.

"Don't you understand, Millie will be a mother to you," Jonas said.

Crockett's Long Trip To Kentucky

"Millie can't take my Maws place!" Crockett insisted.

"I know son, no one can take your Maws place, but Millie can fill a void in our lives," Jonas answered.

"We will all live together in a cabin or over at the big Truitt house," Jonas said.

"Well Paw when will you and Millie get married?" Crockett asked in a more somber tone.

"We have not set an exact date, but in two to three months," Jonas answered.

Jonas hugged Crockett!

"Don't you know I would never abandon you for any woman?" Jonas asked.

"What did Hannah think?" asked Crockett.

"She seemed pleased at the idea," Jonas said.

"This will be a good thing for you, Hannah, and me," Jonas said.

"Don't you know that Millie loves you and Hannah?" Jonas asked.

"Not really," Crockett answered.

"We have two months to get use to the idea, please give her a chance son," Jonas said.

"I will, paw," Crockett said half way smiling.

A few days passed and the weather had been great for the end of November. Jonas and Bill took advantage of the good weather to get as much done as possible on the mill. The main gear had been fashioned and installed on the opposite end of the great water wheel. A number of the support timbers were set and walls were up to the second story on three sides. The floor joists on the second floor were installed except where access was needed to work on the mill apparatus.

The mill stones had arrived in South Shore and Jonas took Bill Thompson to get them. Crockett was in school and missed this trip. The wagon had to be beefed up with heavy timbers to support the weight of two heavy grinding stones. Also a tandem team of mules was used to pull the wagon.

When Jonas and Bill arrived at South Shore the stones were already unloaded and setting on the side of the river. They had been handled carefully it appeared. When Bill saw them he was amazed at the black granite and smoothness of the

Crockett's Long Trip To Kentucky

surface. Grinding furrows were cut in the sides deep toward the center and shallow toward the outer edge. A cross shaped opening was cut in the center of the turn stone and the set stone had a smaller round hole.

"Jonas these things are beautiful, they would make grand tomb stones," Bill said.

Jonas laughed at the idea.

"These stones cost more than some farms, so we must take real good care handling them," Jonas said.

Bill took a step back as if afraid to touch the precious grinding stones.

"Don't be afraid of them Bill, we just can't drop them," Jonas explained.

The grinding stones were round like wheels four feet in diameter and one foot thick. The set stone was marked as weighting 998#, the turn stone was marked as weighting 980#.

"How come that one is heavier?" Bill asked.

"Cause it don't have a cross cut in it, I reckon," Jonas said.

Jonas went in to claim the grinding stones and make provisions to get them loaded.

The owner of the river port had a makeshift crane boom brought out and with help of a couple of hands the stones were loaded into the reinforced wagon on a bed of straw.

Back at school Crockett was beside himself with anticipation of the grinding stones coming. He might as well have gone with Jonas and Bill to get them, because his mind sure was not on school today. Samuel tried to get Crockett's attention back on his studies but even he was not as attentive today.

Excitement was in the air because the mill stone wheels were coming. This made the mill a reality, not just a big wheel standing in a trace next to a partially built building.

It would be late in this December day before Jonas and Bill would get back with the precious cargo. The days were short now and darkness would catch them on the trail.

While Jonas was in the little burg of South Shore, he did a little shopping. He bought a pair of dress gloves each for Millie, and Hannah. He also bought Crockett

Crockett's Long Trip To Kentucky

some store bought britches. He also got Crockett a good skinning knife for his upcoming birthday on the 13th of December.

Jonas and Bill arrived about 8:00 PM back in Truittville with the grinding stones. Most of the little burg was waiting in the Truittville Inn, hoping to finally see the costly stones from Italy.

A loud voice rang out, "Here they are!"

Everyone in the Inn followed Samuel Truitt out in the cold night to see the grinding stones. Jonas held his lantern high and threw back the canvas cover to reveal the shiny black granite wheels.

A hush fell over the entire group.

"They are beautiful," Polly exclaimed.

Everyone there was amazed at the fine grinding stones.

are too pret"ty They to grind corn," someone said.

"I have never seen such beautiful stone," Samuel said.

"They will be used for their purpose," Samuel continued.

"We have the best looking grinding stones in Kentucky," Polly announced.

Crockett stood there indignant!

"Ain't nobody ever seen grinding stones before?" asked Crockett.

"Not this purty," Bill Thompson exclaimed.

"They are purty I reckon," Crockett answered.

"Me and Paw have seen a whole passel of then, ain't we Paw?" Crockett asked.

"You are right son, but these are the finest stones I ever seen," Jonas said.

"The Gerardi family has outdone themselves this time," Jonas said.

By now Millie and Hannah had worked their way over close to the stones.

Millie reached over into the wagon and felt the smooth stones and felt down into one of the carved out grinding grooves.

"Oh! That is sharp!" she exclaimed.

"Be careful, you may skin your finger," Jonas cautioned.

Crockett's Long Trip To Kentucky

Crockett snickered quietly.

I never seen folks act so silly about grinding stones, Crockett thought.

"Bill, we better take the wagon out by the mill and unhitch the mules," Jonas said.

"Yes, I bet you fellers are about frozen," exclaimed Samuel Truitt.

Crockett and some of the other boys followed the wagon out by the mill to help with the mules, so Jonas and Bill could hurry out of the cold night air.

After the animals were cared for Jonas went back to the wagon and retrieved three small packages and stuck them under his heavy coat. The packages were the gifts he had purchased in South Shore.

This day was Friday the 10th of December 1847. Monday would be Crockett's birthday, and a little party had been planned by Millie for after church on Sunday. She was planning to bake a cake just for Crockett, and she had also crocheted him a neck scarf from bright blue yarn.

Millie and Hannah waited for Jonas inside the warm inn, while he tended to the mules. Louisa heated up some fine beef soup, knowing the two men would be hungry and cold.

When Jonas and Bill came into the inn, Millie, Hannah, and Louisa were seated at a large table waiting. Louisa had big bowls of soup and cornbread waiting.

Sunday came and Crockett was wondering if anybody was going to remember his birthday. Well it is not until tomorrow he reasoned.

Jonas, Millie and the others have kept the party a grand secret. They had not said a word. They all gathered at the church for worship the same as usual. When church was over everyone headed to the Truitt Inn for dinner as usual.

Maybe they will remember my birthday in the morning, Crockett thought.

When the surrey arrived at the inn, everyone walked in the inn as usual, except Crockett was delayed because Jonas asked him to put out the weight and tie the horse to it.

Everyone gathered around the center table where a large cake was waiting for David Crockett Whitt. When he came in everyone yelled surprise! Crockett was taken completely by surprise, and stood there in amazement.

Crockett's Long Trip To Kentucky

"Good birthday to you son," Jonas said loudly.

Everyone cheered!

They did not sing "Happy Birthday to you" because; the song had not been composed by the schoolteacher Mildred J. Hill in Louisville, Kentucky until the 27th of June 1859.

Hannah was as excited as Crockett. She gave him a big hug, and ate a huge piece of cake that would fill up a lumberjack.

After dinner was over, Jonas stood and called Crockett over to him. He took out the package that was wrapped in brown paper and tied with twine.

"Crockett you are almost a man, and I am giving you a manly gift," Jonas said. "Even though you have used these before you did not have one of your own," Jonas said as he gave the package to Crockett.

"Thanks Paw," he said as he untied the twine, and slowly unwrapped the present.

Crockett's eyes widened as he gazed upon the shiny new skinning knife.

"This is a wonderful birthday Paw, thanks so much," Crockett said.

Hannah was a little disappointed because it was not her birthday. Jonas called her over and told her that she would have her birthday on the 15th of April.

"I do have a little surprise for you though," Jonas said as he handed her the little package bound like Crockett's present.

Her big hazel eyes sparkled with excitement. She hurriedly opened her gift, and revealed the new pair of dress gloves.

"Oh Paw," she said with glee.

Jonas and the other adults laughed at the little darling.

Crockett went around the room showing his prized skinning knife. Everyone congratulated him for his birthday and the grand present.

Jonas walked Millie home and surprised her with the nice dress gloves he got for her when he purchased Hannah's gloves and Crockett's knife.

"Mister Whitt, I am tired of waiting, I want to set a date for our wedding," Millie said.

Crockett's Long Trip To Kentucky

They looked at the calendar for February 1848 and decided on Sunday February the thirteenth.

"Now that that is decided, let's not grieve ourselves with anticipation," Jonas said.

"Alright darling, now that I know for sure that you will be mine, I can wait," Millie exclaimed.

The work on the mill slowed but continued through December and into the new year of 1848.

Crockett went to school every day that Samuel conducted it. Crockett was amazed at the improvement of his penmanship, and reading ability.

Samuel Truitt had a way of instilling pride into the children as they could visibly see great strides in their education.

Crockett and Samuel both were a bit concerned about Crockett's spelling.

"Don't worry Crockett, it will come around," Samuel said in encouragement.

February came around and Jonas talked to Samuel about a trip into Greenup. They planned their trip to the court house, for February the 8th. 1848.

Samuel and Jonas went together to acquire a marriage license and get a bond placed which was the law. Samuel was needed, to give consent for his daughter Mildred Truitt, to marry Jonas Whitt. A friend of the family, Mister William Corum went the bond for Mildred. Everything went according to plan for the wedding that would be Sunday afternoon the 13th of February 1848.

Elder John Young had been asked to perform the Wedding Ceremony, even though he was almost eighty four years old. Why not as he was still very agile for his age and conducted worship services every Lords Day?

David Crockett Whitt, was over his animosities, and felt alright about his father getting married. He had ample time to get used to the idea. Jonas had talked to Crockett on several occasions in preparing him for this change in his life. Jonas also honored Crockett by asking him to be the best man at the wedding.

Jonas and Millie worked out a plan to move in with the Truitt's until a house could be built next summer. Samuel agreed to give Jonas and Millie a few acres to build on near the mill. Crockett and Hannah would share the upstairs rooms with Mary Elizabeth Truitt, and George W. Truitt. Jonas and Millie would have a room of their own. George W. Truitt was grown and stayed in Lewis County much of the time with relatives.

Not much would change as to the meals; all four in this new little family would eat at the Truitt Inn for now. After the mill contract was fulfilled Jonas would be expected to provide for Millie, and of course the Whitt children.

What a difference a year can make in a person's life. A move to a new land, and now love and marriage is for Jonas. This was a big change for Hannah and Crockett also.

Sunday morning the 13th of February 1848 was here. Elder John Young has prepared for the wedding following the morning worship service. The wedding was an open church wedding and open to whoever wanted to come. Invitations were not sent out but the date had been announced at church the last two Sundays.

After the closing prayer, the unusually large crowd remained for the wedding. Elder Young went to the front of the church directly in front of the pulpit. He raised both arms as a sign for Jonas and Millie to come to the front along with the wedding party. Every one stood as the bride and groom made their way.

Jonas took Millie by the arm and went to Elder Young. Crockett went and stood beside his father. Hannah Whitt and Mary Elizabeth Truitt took their place as bridesmaids beside of Miss Mildred Truitt. Samuel stood behind his daughter as father of the bride.

There was no music as was the custom of the old Baptist. The congregation remained standing until Elder Young waved for all to be seated.

"Who gives this woman to be wed?" Asked Elder Young?

"Her mother and I," said Samuel Truitt.

Samuel turned and walked back to be seated by his wife Polly.

Elder Young took them through a short but very religious ceremony. He had them kneel for most of the wedding ritual. He had them stand and pronounced them man and wife.

Jonas took Millie into his arms and gave her a big, but dignified kiss.

Everyone cheered and the young ladies hurried toward the front in hopes of catching the bride's bouquet.

Crockett's Long Trip To Kentucky

Millie faced the eager group of young ladies. Then she turned her back to them and tossed the bouquet over her shoulder. Hannah and Mary Elizabeth both jumped for the prize. Mary Elizabeth being older and taller out jumped Hannah and retrieved the bouquet. Everyone cheered.

Samuel walked to the front and held up his right arm, and a hush fell over the church. "Thank all of you for being here today to see my Millie marry Mister Jonas Whitt," Samuel said.

Cheers went up from the congregation.

"We are having a reception in about an hour at the Truitt Inn, cake and tea will be provided for all, come and help us celebrate this great occasion," Samuel announced.

Crockett was alright with today's happenings, at least for now. He was trying his best not to resent his new stepmother.

He and Jonas would be moving their things over to the big Truitt house after the party.

Some things, Crockett will just have to use to, Millie thought. She has felt some negative vibrations from Jonas' son. Millie decided to do as Crockett, try to make it work for the benefit of Jonas.

The reception was enjoyed by most everyone on Big White Oak creek. Samuel brought out his finest spirits and a large amount of tea was brewed. Also a grand wedding cake was provided. Banjos, fiddles, and other musical instruments were brought in and a dance began.

Crockett got into the spirit of things and asked Mary Elizabeth Truitt to dance with him. She too was in the spirit of this happy time. She smiled at Crockett and went on the dance floor with him. They had several dances together, before William Randolph Thompson (Bill) cut in on Crockett and occupied Mary Elizabeth's time the rest of the night. Crockett was hurt by Mary and his friend Bill, because he had special feelings for Mary.

Crockett and Jonas moved their things over to the Truitt house after the wedding party. At least Crockett would live under the same roof as Mary Elizabeth. He would have opportunity to win her over to his way of thinking. At least that was his plan.

Crockett's Long Trip To Kentucky

Crockett stayed busy with school and helping Bill and Jonas with the building of the Mill. Mary was always flirting with him, which kept him committed to his plan to capture her heart.

Also at the dance Hannah had flirted with Alfred Thompson so much that he had a dance or two with her. He still considered her a child but she had other ideas in the back of her young mind.

Mary Elizabeth and Hannah were the best of friends and were always together even though Mary was much older.

Everything went well with the living accommodations and things settled down between Crockett and Bill Thompson. They worked well together and with Jonas leading and teaching, the mill project was coming along splendidly.

Spring was coming to Greenup County. The Robins had been back for some time and even a Buzzard had been seen circling high over Big White Oak creek. Some of the early plowing had begun so that potatoes and other early crops could be planted. Tobacco and even lettuce beds had been prepared.

The mill works were in place and almost ready to test. The chimney was being laid up to provide heat on both the first and second floor of the mill. Samuel ordered two potbellied stoves to serve as heat rather than having fire places. He kept telling Jonas that it is time they come out of the dark ages and use modern things. Jonas was not too sure about some modern things.

Alfred Thompson delivered the lumber in a timely manner as Jonas needed it. Hannah always made it a point to bring Alfred a cup of tea and do a little flirting. Alfred enjoyed the attention of this lovely young lady. Mary Elizabeth was a good friend to Crockett and always treated him well. She was a flirt with all the young men, especially Bill. This drove Crockett crazy, even though he tried not let it show. Crockett decided that she was just friendly with everyone and kept Bill as his friend.

The new grist mill looked naked to those that had not seen a mill being built before. The great water wheel and all the workings were still exposed because the siding had not been put on yet. A frame work for the whole thing was in place and even the roof had been applied to keep out the falling weather.

Jonas was getting anxious to test the workings before everything was enclosed. He had built a sluice gate in the water trace upstream of the waterwheel. It was

Crockett's Long Trip To Kentucky

built close to the earth still remaining in the trace. When things were right the last ten feet of earth would be removed. Then the excess stones that had been gathered would be put into the creek to form a partial dam. This would force the creek through the sluice gate and under the twenty foot waterwheel. The water rate through the gate would be used to control the mill workings. In the best mills the waterwheel turned ten revolutions per minute.

The mill workings were built with the ability to adjust. The set stone could be raised or lowered to the miller's preference. The closer the stones are together the finer the flour or corn meal.

The rate of feeding the grain into the mill stones is set by raising the shaker shoe under the hopper. Also the slower the feed the finer the flour or corn mill.

The finer the flour the more power is needed to turn the waterwheel, the slower the milling, the greater the wear on the stones. The excellent granite stones imported from Italy would wear much better than most other mill stones.

The coarser the flour and the faster the mill turns, the more grain is ground. If the grain stop flowing for any reason the mill stone will grind against each other, get over heated, worn and probably be damaged. Everything had to be in perfect adjustment and a miller had to stay in attention while the mill was grinding. Also Jonas had warned Bill and Crockett to stay clear of moving parts. A waterwheel had the power to run the gears and turn the stone. It could also grab an unsuspecting person and crush them to death. The mill parts would be covered as much as possible to protect the miller, once everything was ready.

As Jonas, Crockett, and Bill installed each part, the bearing points had been packed with heavy grease. Jonas had Crockett and Bill turn the great waterwheel by hand while he had observed each moving part and made adjustments. He was feeling confident about the operation of the new Truitt Mill.

The day the water would be released to the waterwheel was coming soon for the first test. There was a real rush of excitement the first time a mill come to life, so everyone was anxious for this day to come.

Jonas knew this mill was built strong and true, he had used iron parts as reinforcement throughout the mill. Richard Whitt had done a splendid job of fabricating the pieces needed for this in his blacksmith shop.

Crockett's Long Trip To Kentucky

Samuel Truitt was excited that a test was coming for his mill. He had relayed to Jonas that he wanted Bill Thompson trained in all aspects of running the mill and maintaining it. William Randolph Thompson would be the miller of Truittville.

Later Jonas would have to show Bill how to lift and turn the turnstone so it could be dressed and also be able to dress the set stone. Even the best of grindstones wore down after extended use. At that point everything would be re-lubricated. Bill would have much to learn about adjustments, and staying safe around so many moving parts. Another thing to learn would be to re-dress the stones which were a skilled chore.

Crockett, Bill, and Jonas worked diligently through the spring and summer on building the mill. Everything was in place for a test run; the earth in the upper section of the mill trace could now be dug out. The last step would be to carry all the rocks to dam up the creek.

Samuel Truitt had every employee muster in to Jonas with picks and shovels. Jonas directed them as to digging out the earth and when it was almost cleared to bed rock the stones were carried out into the creek to build the dam. Crockett and the other boys made a game of it playing in the creek.

Big White Oak Creek began to rise and pour into the trace and build up at the sluice gate. Jonas observed all of this and informed them that more rock was needed in the creek.

The creek was down somewhat because of the dry summer. Jonas would have to come up with something to help the situation because of the low water in the creek.

"Crockett you and the boys go to the barn and fetch all the canvas you can find," Jonas said.

The boys ran to the barn and returned with several pieces of canvas. Jonas instructed them on how to put in a piece at a time over the rock dam and anchor it down with some of the stones. This prevented the water from flowing through the stone dam. This worked splendidly. The water rose to the top of the dam and filled the trace behind the sluice gate.

It was the first week of September 1848, and most everyone on Big White Oak Creek gathered to see the mill come to life. Jonas took corn into the mill and prepared to do the first grind.

Crockett's Long Trip To Kentucky

"Alright boys start opening the sluice gate and let her flow," Jonas hollered to Crockett and Bill.

The gate was raised and water poured through the trace toward the big water wheel. It was the moment of truth. The power of Big White Oak Creek was released to the mill and the great wheel began to move. The mill becomes alive. The wheel turned at the exact speed Jonas wanted and he began to grind corn. Everyone hollered and hooped! Samuel ran into the mill and hugged Jonas with excitement.

During this week most every family brought corn and some even wheat to grind. Jonas did the first and then had Bill Thompson take over to learn the routine of milling. Crockett was there learning and participating.

Millie and Hannah were also excited for the completion and success of the mill. "Paw we should have a party to celebrate the success of your mill," she told Samuel.

Chapter 12
Marriages And Discord.

Samuel thought the idea of a celebration was in order. He decided to have a dance the evening of the last Saturday in September 1848. This would be a harvest dance and a celebration of the completion of Truitt Mill. Samuel sent the word out by word of mouth that on Saturday, September the 25th 5:00 PM the people will come together for thanksgiving and festivities.

Samuel had asked the Elder John Young to be in attendance, even if someone would have to bring him. John Young was an Elder in all respects, Elder by his position as minister in the Baptist church, and he was also an elderly man in his eighties.

Elder Young was pleased and replied that, "Lord willing I will be there."

Samuel was feeling very thankful for all that the Lord has done for his family and all of Big White Oak. Samuel was so pleased to be able to look at the mill and see the great waterwheel turning about ten times every minute. To Samuel this was a dream come true. He thought about all of his accomplishments and gave God credit for all of it. The little town held his name, and in Truittville he had a shoe factory, a Tavern and Inn. He ran the Truitt farm, and was postmaster. He also found time to teach the children. He also practiced medicine. Samuel never attended medical school, but he was an apprentice for some time to a medical doctor. Some folks always referred to Samuel as doctor. Yes the Lord has been gracious to Samuel Truitt and his family, and Samuel knew it.

Jonas, Samuel, Millie, Crockett, and Hannah walked out together into the field to pick a suitable place for a house. Samuel figured over close to the mill, thinking if anything went wrong Jonas would be close by. Jonas and Millie looked and decided back against the hill. The edge of the woods looked better to them.

"What do you all think?" Jonas asked looking at Crockett and Hannah.

"I think back at the hill, cause it will be cool in summer," Hannah said.

Crockett's Long Trip To Kentucky

"I see a fine house in the edge of the woods," replied Crockett.

He remembered Jonas and big brother John Bunyon picking a place to build a cabin back on the Indian Creek Farm. He remembered Jonas saying, "I see a cabin right there in the middle of a Poplar grove.

"I see a fine house in the edge of the woods," Jonas said laughing.

"I see it too," replied Millie.

"Where Paw, I can't see it," replied Hannah.
Everyone laughed!

"That settles it, I am starting to see it too," said Samuel.

The Mill finished and running on an even keel, Jonas put forth his next effort to building a home. He drew up a plan and had Millie interject her ideas into it. He made up an order for lumber and gave it to Alfred Thompson.

As usual Hannah was front and center anytime Alfred was around. She made sure he knew about the celebration and harvest dance coming up next Saturday.

Crockett also talked about it in front of Mary Elizabeth Truitt. He wanted to dance with her again and maybe get a little commitment from her to be his girlfriend.

September the 25th came around quickly, and it was time for the folks to gather for thanksgiving and celebration.

People were already coming in from their homes and farms. One of Elder John Young's neighbors agreed to bring him in his buggy to make sure he could attend. The men were wearing their best clothes and the ladies wore their best southern gowns. Everyone was in a festive mood.

After a short talk and long prayer from the Elder, Samuel stood up and gave a short talk about how gracious God has been to the people on Big White Oak Creek. He pointed out that the mill was a great addition to the area. He commended Jonas and others who contributed to the completion of the mill. He also cited the fact that this was a great growing summer. He mentioned that some

Crockett's Long Trip To Kentucky

farmers grew wheat for the first time by faith that there would be a mill to grind it. He offered up a short prayer of thanksgiving and then said, "Where is the fiddler?"

The party was started with the first chord of music and a dance began. Crockett headed for the fair lady Mary Elizabeth Truitt, and escorted her to the dance floor. They had two or three dances and she said she wanted to sit down. Crockett took her to be seated and stood beside her while she sat. William Randolph Thompson saw Mary and came and stood in front of her.

"Miss Mary may I have this dance?" Bill asked in a formal tone.

Mary rose to her feet and accepted graciously! Bill escorted Mary out to where the dancers were and took her into his arms. Crockett stood there indignant. His anger rose up from the tips of his toes to the top of his head. His face became a glowing red. He would not be able to stand here and watch his dream girl dance away the evening with that Bill Thompson. Crockett knew he better leave or something bad might happen. He headed over to the mill and sat in a secluded place to watch the water flow through the trace. This had become Crockett's space for thinking and daydreaming. Crockett slowly cooled his anger, and tried to rationalize that Bill and Mary were just friends as was he friends to both of them.

Crockett sat there for over an hour listening to the music, and thinking. He let his mind wander even back to Tazewell County, and to all that he had done in his short life. After his anger cooled, he felt some guilt so he decided to pray. He prayed out his thoughts to the Lord and asked for forgiveness. Crockett felt much better, so he decided to go back to the party and maybe eat something and visit some with all the folks. Crockett noticed Hannah had corralled Alfred Thompson and they were dancing gleefully. He also noticed that Mary was dancing with one of the other boys. He felt much better about the situation, so he settled down and halfway enjoyed the rest of the evening.

The fall gave way to winter, and Crockett once again enjoyed the teachings of Samuel Truitt. His penmanship was much improved as was his spelling. He learned arithmetic and could figure wages, volume of containers, square feet and even fractions. He also learned the pleasure of reading a book. Samuel was well pleased with his progress.

Crockett's Long Trip To Kentucky

Mary Elizabeth Truitt went to school this being her last year. She would be turning seventeen and would finish her education at home learning female things from mother Polly and her big sisters.

With the end of January 1849 came the big news that gold was discovered in California by James Marshall a Mormon. He discovered it at Sutter's Mill just lying in the creek. The Gold rush was on; many folks from all walks of life sold all they had and headed to California. Even a few folks from Greenup County, Kentucky would go and try to become wealthy. Many people would lose everything and some even their lives.

Crockett got enthused about the idea, but Jonas showed him the folly of it all. He showed Crockett some Newspapers with folks being killed and becoming destitute for following crazy ventures like this. He even quoted from Proverbs some passages about people trying to run after wealth. Crockett understood, but still thought the adventure would be fun. He decided to stay and learn some more good things from his friend, Samuel Truitt.

In February 1849 news came that the Mexican war was ended with a treaty and a payment of fifteen million dollars to Mexico. Mexico ceded five hundred thousand square miles of great land to the United States. This would create another land rush.

Crockett thought, I am living in exciting times. He had heard so many stories of the western lands. Coming to Kentucky had been a big adventure, he couldn't imagine what it would be like to travel over two thousand miles and search for gold.

The spring of 1849 was upon Greenup County once again. Folks were busy with farming duties, and Jonas was in the process of finishing the new house. It would be good to move out of the crowded Truitt home. Crockett would still be able to see Mary Elizabeth Truitt every day.

One day Crockett was down the creek about a mile and a half. He saw Mister Quillen trying to get his little flock of sheep to cross the creek. Sheep are afraid of water and will not willingly go into it even if it is shallow. Crockett stood there and watched the man try one thing then another. The sheep were only getting more afraid.

Crockett's Long Trip To Kentucky

"Mister Quillen, I see you are having trouble getting the sheep to this side of the creek," Crockett said.

"Sheep are the dumbest critters on God's green earth," Mister Quillen uttered.

"I never seen it happen, but I heard of a feller back home in Virginia in the same predicament," Crockett said.
"What did he do?" asked Mister Quillen.

"He picked out the leader of the flock and tried to drag it in the water but the dang thing turned around, so he jest drug it across hind part first," Crockett said.

"What happened next?" asked Mister Quillen?
"Well all them other sheep looked and seen their leader backing across the river, so they turned around and backed across the river too," Crockett exclaimed.

Mister Quillen fell to his knees with laughter.

"That is the funniest story I ever heard," exclaimed Mister Quillen.

Crockett laughed with him.

"You may have an idea there son, at least part of it," laughed Mister Quillen.

Mister Quillen picked out the leader of the flock, put a rope around its neck and led it across the creek, all the others followed.

"Thank you Crockett, I would have loved to have seen all them Virginia sheep backing across that river," laughed Mister Quillen.

Jonas received a letter from his brother James stating that he has sold the Dismal Creek farm to Thomas Brown as part of settling the estate of their late father Hezekiah Whitt. Jonas would receive a seventh which would be Twenty-five Dollars, and also mentioned in the letter was John Bunyon Whitt. James wanted Jonas and John to go to the Greenup County Court House and sign over their part of the farm to Thomas Brown and then their money would be free and clear.

Also about this time Jonas received a letter from John Madden Stephenson and

Crockett's Long Trip To Kentucky

Emma Whitt Stephenson asking for some assistance on buying a farm in Tazewell County. John was his son in law and of course Elizabeth was his daughter.

So Jonas went to the Greenup County Court House on the 17th of August 1849 and signed over his part of the Dismal farm to Thomas Brown. They both were able to cash their drafts now free and clear, after John Bunyon took care to do the same.

Jonas was back in the court house on the 19th of August 1849 before the justices making record, giving substance from his wealth to John Madden Stephenson and Emma his daughter on the purchase of a farm in Tazewell County, Virginia.

David Crockett Whitt and Henrietta (Hannah) Whitt were both growing and maturing into young adults. Hannah Whitt was love struck by Alfred Thompson; she would simply die if she didn't get him for a husband. Crockett felt about the same about Mary Elizabeth Truitt. The only problem was that Mary was a flirt and her strongest feelings were for William Randolph Thompson.

In the spring of 1850 Hannah and Mary E. Truitt cooked up the idea for a double wedding in June. Hannah was more or less a child, but seemed to know her mind, and was in love with Alfred Thompson from the first time she saw him.
Mary Elizabeth Truitt still flirted with Crockett when Bill was not around. This added fuel to Crockett's jealousy against his one-time friend William (Bill) Randolph Thompson. Bill Thompson was Fifteen years senior to young Crockett, but was not a big man physically. Crockett was only thirteen but tall and strong for his age.

Jonas had stayed busy with his new house, going to Greenup on business, and working around the mill. Also he had a young wife to keep up with as he was senior to Millie by twenty-six years. Jonas knew something was going on with Crockett but figured it was just growing pains!

Hannah and Alfred were going to get married with William Randolph Thompson and Mary Elizabeth if permission was gained from the girls respective fathers. Mary and Hannah thought a double wedding would be great. They even decided to all live together in one house and share the cost.

When Crockett heard these plans he was in an almost uncontrollable state of mind. He went out into the woods and took out his frustrations by lifting big rocks over his head and working out. He had learned to control anger by doing this. He also had developed a strong physical body for his young age of thirteen.

Jonas gave Hannah permission even though he felt she was too young. Samuel also gave Mary Elizabeth permission and asks Jonas to go the bond for both girls. Jonas agreed and went to the Greenup Courthouse on Wednesday June 12, 1850 and placed bond for both girls to be wed.

David Crockett Whitt could not believe Mary was really going to marry Bill Thompson and Jonas was even going the bond. The wedding was only a week away set for June 15th. 1850 and Crockett had some adjusting to do. Another thing Crockett could not believe was that Jonas was letting Hannah get married the same day. She would be a child bride.

On Friday June 14th 1850 Crockett decided to talk to Mary Elizabeth Truitt about this wedding farce. He intended to tell her he loved her deeply and would ask her to call off the wedding. He figured if he talked her out of it even Hannah would put her wedding off.

He mustered up enough courage to confront Mary. He was not well received. He laid his heart on the line and spoke softly and pleaded for her to put off her wedding to Bill. She became obstinate!

"You silly boy," Mary told him.

"You are just immature and have no idea of what love is," she continued.

"I have loved you from the day I first looked upon your beautiful face," Crockett said.

"You need to grow up and find yourself a little girlfriend," Mary answered.

"I am betrothed to be wed tomorrow and you should not be here talking to me like this, go away and leave me alone," Mary said in a very hurtful way.

Crockett's countenance fell! Crockett turned his head quickly and ran off toward the woods to hide the tears streaming down his face. He ran out to do his therapy

Crockett's Long Trip To Kentucky

of rock lifting to try and calm down. Crockett had never in his life felt so rejected by his father and by the girl he loved. His anger did not subside but grew toward Bill Thompson.

Even though Crockett was tall and very strong for a thirteen year old, he knew the man Bill Thompson could whip him in a fair fight. Crockett thought if he softened up Bill, he had a chance to give him a good whipping. That is what he wanted to do at this very moment. Crockett knew Bill Thompson was always in the barn about this time every evening taking care of all the horses. Crockett looked around and found himself a club and sneaked into the barn. Bill was not there yet so Crockett found himself a hiding place in the shadows.

In a few minutes Bill Thompson came into the barn right on time. Crockett waited until Bill went into a stall and had his back turned to him. Crockett came out of the shadows in a rage and hit Bill over the head with a vicious blow. To Crockett's surprise Bill Thompson crumpled to the straw covered barn floor.

Reality struck Crockett!

"What have I done?" he thought.

"My God, I have killed an innocent man!" Crockett said out loud.

Crockett ran for Jonas, and just so happened Jonas was on his way toward the barn.
Crockett ran to Jonas and stood before him.

"Paw I have done a terrible thing, I killed Bill Thompson!" Crockett said in a whisper.

"What am I to do?" Crockett asked in desperation.

Jonas stood there for a moment in shock!

"What did you do Crockett?" Jonas asked.

"I was in such agony over Bill and Mary I hit Bill in the head with a club," Crockett confessed.

Crockett's Long Trip To Kentucky

"He is lying in the end stall in the barn, Paw I am so sorry, I only wanted to give him a good whipping," Crockett continued.

Jonas regained his composure and thought quickly.
"Crockett did Bill know you struck him?" Jonas asked?

"No Paw I don't believe he knew what hit him," Crockett said.

"Crockett you have to leave now or face the noose, you go and saddle Jake and head to your Uncle James' in Virginia," Jonas said.

"Do not write nor visit any of our kin on the way there, get out of Kentucky as quick as you can," Jonas continued.

Jonas gave him a twenty dollar gold piece, and Crockett slipped out on Jake and rode away quietly down the creek toward Tygart Creek. Crockett being only thirteen and a half, with only the clothes on his back was running for his life.

Jonas hurried to the barn to check on Bill Thompson! As Jonas came close to the end stall he saw William Randolph Thompson sprawled out on the barn floor. He went close and felt for a pulse. Great Scott, Bill is still alive.

Jonas rose up and quickly looked about. He saw a loose timber just above the stall. Jonas hurriedly got up and took the timber down and laid it beside Bill. He looked around quickly for the club, and it is nowhere in sight. The cover up was in place so Jonas ran to get Doctor Samuel Truitt and others to give aid to Bill.

Samuel grabbed his little doctor bag, and headed for the barn followed closely by Jonas and everyone that heard the news. It was just getting dark so the ladies followed with a lantern.
"My God, that timber must have fallen on him, I told one of the boys to get that thing down just the other day," Samuel said.

Samuel got down close and turned Bill over on his back and looked him over the best he could in the dim light.

"Jonas we got to get him in the house so we can minister to him," Samuel said.

Crockett's Long Trip To Kentucky

"I agree, everybody get hold of him and let's carry him quickly to the house," Jonas said.

As they picked him up Bill Thompson let out a big groan.

"Bill, you hold on, we will have you in the house in just a minute," Samuel said.

Bill grunted!

They got Bill laid down on the bed and lit three oil lamps. Samuel poured some water from the pitcher into the bowl on the washstand. He took a washcloth and wet it and began to wash Bill's face. Bill's body began to quicken as though he was coming back to life. Bill opened his eyes slowly, and tried to look around. "Where am I?" Bill asked in a slurred voice.

"Just lay quietly Bill, you are here in my house, you were in an accident," Samuel reassured him.

Mary Elizabeth Truitt was standing close by still partly in shock.

"Paw is my sweetheart going to be alright?" Mary asked.

"I think he will live, and I think he will come out of it alright," Samuel answered.

"Now everyone clear out and let him get some air," Samuel said as he loosened his shirt and ministered to him.

Samuel got in his bag and opened a little bottle of smelling salts, put a little on the tip of a rag and stuck it close to Bill's nose. Bill shook his head in protest.

"Doc what are you doing to me?" Bill asked in a loud voice.

Samuel chuckled as he held up three fingers to Bill!

"How many fingers do you see?" Samuel asked.

"Three," Bill answered.

Crockett's Long Trip To Kentucky

"Who are you marrying tomorrow?" Samuel asked.

"My sweet Mary Elizabeth," Bill answered.

"You are going to be just fine!" Samuel said.

"My head is a busting Doc," Bill said.

"I will get you some headache powder, and you will be fine by in the morning," Samuel assured him.

Samuel got Bill something for his headache and to make him rest. After Mary gave him a kiss everyone left and she blew out all the lamps except for one on the bed stand. Samuel told Mary to sit quietly and watch Bill for a while, while he slept.

"Wake him up in about two hours and make him talk to you," Doctor Truitt said.

The cover up that Jonas orchestrated seemed to be working fine. Crockett could have stayed Jonas thought. Then he had second thoughts, I guess it is best for him to go back to Virginia.

By now Crockett is going down the Tygart and almost to the Coal Creek trail to the Ohio River. He pushed Jake pretty hard and now slowed to a steady gait of about six miles per hour.

Crockett's head is clearing and he comes up with a plan for a route back to Tazewell County, Virginia. He has decided to swim Jake across the Ohio River, then rest until morning. Then he will go up river to just above the mouth of Big Sandy and cross back in to Virginia near Kenova.

As Crockett started down the hollow toward the river he let Jake walk to rest him before the Ohio crossing. Thank goodness the summer was here and the water level was down. Jake would be able to wade much of the way across. (There were no dams on the river in 1850)

As Crockett came up on the river he dismounted and walked Jake to the edge of the river and surveyed the situation. Jake's ears were standing up and his nostrils

Crockett's Long Trip To Kentucky

flared. Jake could sense that he was going swimming.

Crockett mounted up once again and said to Jake, "No time like the present old friend."

Jake made a little protest whinny! Crockett patted Jake to reassure him.

Crockett guided Jake into the waters of the great Ohio River. Jake waded about one third of the way before the bottom dropped off. When Jake started to swim Crockett took his feet from the stirrups and stretched out on Jakes back to take a little weight off but held on to the saddle horn with both hands.

"You are doing just fine Jake, you are a good boy," Crockett encourages!

Jake is a fine horse, even in the middle of the Ohio River, he stayed calm and kept to his task. Jake kept up a steady swim, slow and easy. About one third way from the northern bank the bottom came back up under his feet, and he began walking the bottom again.

Crockett pulled himself back into the saddle and kept encouraging Jake. Where Jake came out of the water the bank was a little steep, but Jake carried Crockett right up to the top without stopping. Now they were out on good level ground in the State of Ohio.

Crockett petted Jake on his neck and dismounted. Crockett kept praising Jake for doing so good! When Crockett talked to him Jake turned his head toward him and rolled his eyes to see Crockett. It was pretty dark but Jake could see pretty well.

Crockett and Jake were both dripping wet, and the night air seemed extra cool. Crockett decided it would be better if they traveled on for a while. He knew that they would dry quicker traveling. Crockett knew that you don't ride a horse hard, and put him away wet. Jake was not a spring chicken any more, or should I say spring horse?

Crockett guided Jake north for a short time until Jake found the road that traveled basically east and west. Crockett turned Jake up the road to the east. They traveled about an hour toward Hanging Rock and found an isolated barn. Crockett checked it out and found that it had some hay for Jake, and a good place for him to lie down until morning. Crockett unsaddled Jake and hung up the blanket. He

Crockett's Long Trip To Kentucky

made some hay available to Jake and he lay down to get some rest. Crockett figured it to be about midnight. Crockett drifted off to sleep and Jake munched on the hay.

Morning came quickly for Crockett. He jumped to his feet when he came to his senses. The sun was already shining. Crockett took a peek out the barn door but saw no one. Next he put the almost dry blanket and saddle on Jake and led him out.

As he looked east he could see the big hill and cliff protruding almost to the river.

"Jake we are almost to Hanging Rock," Crockett said as he petted the important anima.

Crockett knew that without Jake he would be sunk.

As Crockett looked at the beautiful Hanging Rock the sun seemed to line the south edge with bright gold light. Should change the name to Shining Rock this morning, Crockett thought. Then Crockett thought about the history of this place, Indians have been coming here to Hanging Rock for years. From the summit the river could be viewed several miles both east and west. Even the great Chiefs, Tecumseh, and the white man turned Indian Blue Jacket, were known to visit this place.

Crockett had a hunger in his stomach so he began to look for something he could eat. Off the road about fifty yards to the north was a little grove of paw-paw bushes. They were not ripe as they should be. There was an abundance of fruit on the higher branches, as the animals had eaten all the low Paw Paws. Crockett rode up to the bushes and picked from the back of Jake. He filled his saddle bag with the fruit and Jake even picked himself a treat or two.

"Kinda sour ain't they boy?' Crockett asked Jake.

Crockett began to pass a few folks on the road and came up on the newly founded town of Ironton. Ironton was a natural shipping port, because of the iron smelted in the surrounding Ohio hills. Crockett rode Jake through the burg nonchalantly not wanting to attract attention to himself. On the Far East end of Ironton, Crockett came to a creek. He dismounted and let Jake drink his fill of the clear water. (This creek is now called Ice Creek.)

Crockett kept thinking back to the events of yesterday. If there was some way to

Crockett's Long Trip To Kentucky

take it all back he would do it in a minute. Then the dread of being chased by a posse hung heavy on his mind. Could he ever be forgiven by the Lord and by his Paw, he kept asking himself.

Crockett wondered what folks thought in Truittville? What did Mary Elizabeth Truitt think? What did his sister Hannah think?

Crockett set himself a goal of crossing back across the Ohio River into Virginia before dark. (Now West Virginia.) He wanted to cross into (present day Kenova) just to the east side of Big Sandy River. He was thinking about what Jonas told him, get out of Kentucky as quick as possible, and back to Virginia. He was out of Kentucky, now he had to cross the big river one more time. He did not look forward to it, but doing it in daylight should be better.

Meanwhile back in Truittville, William Randolph Thompson was doing fine except for having a sore head. He and Mary talked and decided to keep their wedding date. Alfred Thompson and Hannah were relieved that everything was still set and there would be double wedding at the Baptist Church for this afternoon. Hannah asked Jonas where Crockett was this morning.

"Not sure, he wanted to take an adventure trip," Jonas said.

"He was a little hurt at Mary Elizabeth and Bill so he thought it would be a good time to see Kentucky and visit some of his kin," Jonas continued.

Jonas kept to that story all day as others asked. Not too many were surprised that Crockett left for a while.

Both Hannah and Mary married their beaus this day and would spend the night in the Truitt Inn. Tomorrow both couples would move into a little cabin together. They thought for now, this would be less costly and besides that both couples were best of friends.

A reception was held at the inn after the wedding, and folks were ready for a dance and celebration. Jonas went along as though nothing had happened, even though he had a heavy heart. Now Jonas and Millie had an empty nest at least for now. Millie had not become pregnant as yet.

Crockett's Long Trip To Kentucky

Back in Ohio, Crockett and Jake were getting close to the planned river crossing. He sat on the river bank for a spell and let Jake rest and do some grazing on the lush grass. They were right across from the mouth of Big Sandy River. This area of Ohio was called South Point because it was the southernmost point in the state of Ohio.

It was getting late in the afternoon of Saturday the 16th of June 1850, and Crockett waded Jake back into the waters of the big river. Crockett was about an eighth of a mile up river from the mouth of Big Sandy River. He could see a few houses on the Kenova, Virginia shore.(Present day West Virginia.)(Kenova established 1857)

David Crockett Whitt did as before and let Jake take his time with the crossing. He continued talking to his good friend. Jake seemed to have them on Virginia soil in no time at all. (Now West Virginia.)

Crockett and Jake rode by a few homes and continued up the east side of Big Sandy for about an hour. They came up on a nice level area in the Big Sandy Valley, and it was almost dark again. (Near Present day Prichard, West Virginia.) The area had lush grass and looked like a good place to spend the night. He unsaddled Jake and hobbled him. Then he hung up the wet blanket and saddle on a lower limb of a tree. Crockett gathered some leaves and straw and made himself a bed. He next gathered some firewood and lit himself a fire by flint and steel which he hastily grabbed when he left Truittville. It was Paw Paws for supper, and hopefully he could settle down tomorrow and get some real food.

Crockett got warm by his little fire and dried out his clothes. Jake's blanket would be dry by in the morning. Jake grazed peacefully nearby.

Crockett had no way of knowing things were fine back in Truittville. William Randolph Thompson was not dead. He was actually enjoying his wedding night, as was Hannah and Alfred Thompson.

Jonas prayed for his beloved son, David Crockett Whitt.

Crockett and his horse Jake were worn out and the good night's sleep was refreshing. Crockett was not so on edge this morning when he awoke. He was in Virginia, even though it was about one hundred fifty miles to Uncle James' in Tazewell County.

Crockett's Long Trip To Kentucky

Crockett was hungry and needed some supplies, so he felt safe in stopping at the next little burg. He needed a good man sized meal and a night in a good bed, and Jake could use some rest and a fill of oats. Crockett put the blanket on Jake and saddled up.

"Don't worry old friend, no big rivers to swim today," Crockett said.

Jake rolled his big brown eyes at Crockett.

Crockett guided Jake on up the Big Sandy on the Virginia side toward Fort Gay. (Now Fort Gay, West Virginia.) Crockett remembered that he and Jonas had looked across from Louisa, Kentucky when they came through back in 1847. Fort Gay is directly across the river from Louisa. And this is where the Tug and Levisa forks merge to form the Big Sandy.

Hopefully there will be a store and maybe a place to spend the night. He had the twenty dollar gold piece that Jonas gave him and that would be plenty to get him and Jake back to Baptist Valley in Tazewell County. He just needed to be careful and not let someone steal it from him. The only weapon he had was the skinning knife he got for his last birthday. He would have to stay alert and not be too trusting of strangers, especially on the trail.

Chapter 13
Salvation And Trouble On The Tug Fork

Back in Truittville, Jonas got off to himself and wrote a letter to his brother James Whitt in Baptist Valley, Virginia. Jonas wanted to be off to himself so that he could use the letter to inform Crockett that Bill Thompson was alive and well. He also told of the cover up, and how it made everything look like an accident. The letter also stated that Crockett had a second chance at a good life and should take it by never raising a hand to another person. The letter also told of Hannah marrying Alfred Thompson, and Bill Thompson marrying Mary Elizabeth Truitt. The letter also had the regular greetings and questions about the kin folks in Tazewell County.

Jonas sealed the letter and took it over to Samuel at the Truittville Post Office about the time the post rider was due through. Jonas paid the postage and the rider came through while Jonas was still there. The letter was on its way, but it would do Crockett no good until he could see it in a few weeks.

Crockett and Jake travel on up the Big Sandy until they reached Fort Gay late in the afternoon. Crockett saw a mercantile and also a tavern with rooms on the second floor. He guides Jake to the hitching rail in front of the mercantile, dismounted and tied Jake to the rail.

"You wait right here old boy, I will be out shortly," Crockett said to Jake.

Jake gave him one of those looks, like yeah sure!

"I promise," Crockett said as he turned to go into the store.

Crockett went in and found the bare necessities, and gathered them up. He got a canteen, blanket, piece of canvass about 10 feet by 10 feet. He also got a frying pan, some lard, salt, pepper, an eating fork and a fishing line and hooks. He gathered a few other items of food and two sticks of candy; one for him and one for Jake.

After paying for the goods, Crockett checked on a room for the night and also

Crockett's Long Trip To Kentucky

about livery for Jake. He was told that a room, supper, and bath could be had for a dollar, and Jake could have oats and care in the barn for thirty five cents. Crockett decided to take him up on it because both of them were tired and dirty. Crockett took his stuff up to the room and then took Jake over to the livery stable for the night. He decided to save the candy until later after supper, when he would check on his good friend Jake.

Crockett ate a big supper of cornbread, brown beans and fried potatoes. For dessert he had a fried apple pie. After supper Crockett went over to see how Jake was faring. He had been eating oats and corn. He seemed to be doing just fine. Crockett greeted him and fed him the sweet stick of candy. Crockett petted and talked to him awhile and went back over to get a bath and good night's sleep.

Crockett was so tired he slept like a log, and awoke early the next morning. He had a big breakfast and carried his supplies to the livery stable. Jake came running up to the gate, as soon as he saw Crockett.

"Good morning Jake," Crockett said.

Jake did a little side step in excitement. He was really glad to see someone he knew. Crockett petted him a little and put on the dry blanket, and saddled him up. Jake was anxious to get started on the days adventures Crockett was taking him on.

Crockett had talked to a couple different men at the inn and they both gave him basic directions back to Tazewell County via the Tug Fork. They both explained that the trail was rugged but simple. Both men said that you just follow the river. Both mentioned that it was a winding and crooked river stuck right between the hills. Both men also warned him that road bandits sometimes robbed unsuspecting folks.

One of the men wanted to know why he was traveling by himself. Crockett told him he was on an adventure trip and heading back home.

Crockett mounted Jake and headed up the Tug. He would be getting away from the more traveled trails and roads. It was a shorter way back if you could fly a straight course like a crow. But Crockett would find out that the river ran in all directions but mostly southeast.

Crockett's Long Trip To Kentucky

He rode for about a half a day and stopped to eat a bite and give Jake a rest. This stopping off place was near present day Glenhays, West Virginia. The road was not a busy route as was the Levisa fork road in Kentucky. This made Crockett feel safer in one respect. Jake grazed for about forty five minutes and Crockett ate a bag lunch prepared for him at the inn. Crockett had Jake moving on down the trail toward Tazewell County once again. The weather was nice, but a little hot.

In late afternoon, after crossing a big hill, Crockett came to a flat river bottom. Grass was good here and the river looked like it could produce some fish for supper. This place was near present day Crum, West Virginia.

Crockett stopped for the day. He unsaddled Jake and hobbled him. He set up his canvas as a lean too and put all of his gear under it. He gathered fire wood and made a fire place with a circle of stones. He gathered the worms he found. He looked around and decided he was camp ready. Next Crockett dug out his fishing line and hooks. Then he looked for a suitable pole to cut. He settled on one and cut it with his skinning knife. Next he flopped over a few more rocks and logs for worms. Having everything needed he headed down to a hole in the river just below an eddy. The river was pretty clear but gave off an emerald green color because it was lined on both sides by green bushes and trees. Also poison oak and Virginia reaper vines grew everywhere.

Crockett eased up to the edge of the Tug and tossed in his offering for his first fish. Wham! The pole bent and Crockett set the hook. Out of the river came a flopping small mouth bass. It landed back in the weeds where it came to rest. Crockett pounced on it and put it on a forked stick he had just cut. He baited up again and tossed it back into the depths of the water. He moved it a time or two and tossed it up stream a little. It drifted with the current to just in front of him. Wham! Something knocked its socks off. Crockett set the hook on the second fish and gave a yank. A fat small mouth about fifteen inches long was in the weeds. Once again Crockett moved swiftly to put it on the branch. Crockett fished for a little while longer and caught one more nice fish.

He would have fish for supper and one for breakfast he thought. Crockett had diverted his thoughts off of why he was traveling. After supper and cleanup the agony returned. Why did I kill my one time friend? Why did I allow myself to fall into such trouble? Why did I have to disappoint Paw and the family? Crockett kept

Crockett's Long Trip To Kentucky

asking himself these questions, then the tears began to flow. He felt so alone and hated.

Then he remembered his religious training and knew he had at least one friend as the Holy Spirit spoke to him. Crockett had been humbled by his great mistake, and he remembered the Lord would always listen and was always ready to forgive. Crockett started praying silently and then out loud to Jesus to please forgive him and give him peace. He asked the Lord to take over his life and do with him as he would. Crockett felt an unusual warmth envelope him and a sense of peace soothed his soul. This was the conversion of David Crockett Whitt on the banks of Tug fork in the summer of 1850.

Crockett slept like a baby and woke up feeling altogether different this morning. He shut his eyes and prayed for the Lord to be with him today and protect him as he traveled.

Crockett got up and put his clothes on and walked out to where Jake was grazing.

"Good morning Jake, did you get a good night's rest old boy?" Crockett asked.

Jake shook his head back and forth as if to say he did.

This made Crockett laugh and put a smile on his face.

"Jake you are some hoss!" Crockett said.

Crockett ate the biggest fish he had saved from last night, and broke camp. He got Jake saddled up and all his gear tied on.

"Alright boy lets head up the river," Crockett said.

Jake started to trot with his head turned steep to the left side like a proud thoroughbred, which he pretty much was.

"Show off, let's just go," Crockett said.

They had traveled about a half a mile and came up on a little village, by the name of Crum. It was mostly a few scattered cabins and a little church. A few folks were

Crockett's Long Trip To Kentucky

about. Crockett nodded his head to each person he passed. He saw three old fellers sitting on the steps of an old weathered storehouse. They were chewing tobacco and spinning yarns, Crockett guessed. This looked like a friendly place. But today the whole world looked favorable to Crockett.

Traveling today went well, the terrain was not too objectionable and Jake kept a good pace. They stopped for a little rest in the early afternoon and Crockett let Jake drink from a creek that fed the Tug. Crockett chewed on some hardtack and some strips of jerky. They had come by a few scattered cabins near Stone Coal, and stopped near present day Stepptown. (Present day names.)

Today Crockett did not dwell on the grief of his past sins, but still wondered what was going on back in Truittville. He decided if a posse did catch up with him he would go willingly to the punishment due him. He would not hurt anyone trying to bring him to justice. Yet he would do as Jonas taught him about self-defense if he was confronted by some evil person. Jonas had always instructed him never to bluff, but take whatever action needed to defend himself and his property from evil people.

Crockett camped in a little bottom near the river and did some more fishing for his supper. He was lucky to catch some sunfish, and big red eyes, and gave God thanks for providing for him. Crockett noticed himself talking to God as a friend!

Crockett noticed the valley was getting narrower as he went deeper into the mountain region. It reminded him of the area where Dismal farm was located in the Levisa Valley. The Tug was different in that it went in all directions. The river meandered to the left, right, and sometimes traveled back toward Fort Gay. It was a crooked river.

The trail went about like the river, up and down and around boulders and other obstructions.

"I see why Paw took us down Levisa with our wagon," Crockett thought out loud.

Next day Crockett and Jake traveled on through the area now called Kermit. The Tug Valley spread out again and a nice level area lay out before Crockett. By late in the day Crockett had traveled to another little spread in the Tug Valley. He would spend the night near present day Naugatuck, West Virginia.

Crockett's Long Trip To Kentucky

Crockett noticed the further he traveled up the Tug, the less folks were saw. He also was aware that danger could be waiting around the next bend. He slept more lightly and paid more attention to his surroundings. This area was pure wilderness. Crockett even heard a panther scream during the night. He heard the hoots of an owl, and little rumblings in the woods round about. Crockett got up and built up his fire, then he brought Jake over and tied him on a long rope closer to the fire. He was on edge, but knew this was good to be a little afraid. This kept his senses sharp.

Back in Truittville, Jonas' nephew James G. Whitt son of Richard Whitt showed up. James G. told his Uncle Jonas that he and his Paw had a difference. Richard sent him to visit Crockett and help Jonas for a spell. Jonas made him welcome but explained that Crockett was also gone on an adventure trip.

"Did you and Crockett have a difference Uncle Jonas?" James G. asked.

"No not really, Crockett just wanted to go on an adventure trip and do some visiting, I thought he may show up down to your place," Jonas continued.

"We ain't seen him," replied James G. Whitt.

"Well I'm sure he is fine," Jonas answered.

"You can stay with us for a spell, but you will have to carry your weight," Jonas said.

"I will sir, I would like to learn a little about the mill and how to grind the grain," James G. said.

"I think that can be arranged, Bill Thompson can always use a young man to help," Jonas said.

The little cabin up the creek was staying busy with the two newly wed couples all living together. Millie told Jonas that trouble in paradise was on its way.

"Two families just can't live in harmony in such a little cabin," Millie said.

A notice was sent out to every family on Big White Oak Creek that the 1850

Crockett's Long Trip To Kentucky

Census was going to be taken. Every family in the area was to report to the Truittville Post Office in the near future and give a report of family.

James G. Whitt, Son of Richard, Devil Dick Whitt was counted with Jonas and Mildred (Millie) Whitt. (1850 Census) The four Thompson's living up the creek in the little cabin gave their report, and Hannah Whitt Thompson felt that she should raise her age somewhat. She knew she was too young to be married, but Kentucky had no limit of age. She stated that she was 19, even though she was only about 13.(1850 Census) (1860 Census she stated her age at 23.)

Alfred Thompson, Hannah Thompson, William Randolph Thompson and Mary Elizabeth Thompson reported that they were all living in the same house. (1850 census)

Jonas was very concerned about Crockett, but the only thing he could do was to pray. He hoped that he would get there safe and get the letter he sent. Then he would be free to send an answer back to Kentucky. But for now Crockett thought he was running away from murder, even though all is well in Truittville.

Back on the Tug Crockett woke up the next morning a little more focused on his surroundings. Jake was looking at him as if to say, "You going to lay there all day?"

Crockett got up, broke camp, and he headed up the little road Things seemed pretty normal until Crockett saw a horseman who appeared to be waiting on the trail ahead. Crockett's heart began to race as he realized this man must be an outlaw. Crockett kept up his same speed and showed no alarm but became very focused on the situation. Jake sensed trouble too.

Crockett whispered a prayer for God to be with him, and rode on toward the man. Crockett could see a rifle across the saddle. When Crockett got within speaking distance, the rough looking man spoke.

"Howdy thar sonny," where you headed?

"Hello sir, just going to visit some family," Crockett answered.

Crockett started to ride past the rider, but stopped when the man hollered, "Wait

Crockett's Long Trip To Kentucky

a minute sonny."

Crockett stopped Jake right in front of the man only a few feet away. Crockett could see the man was dirty with un-kept hair and beard. His yellow teeth cast off a breath that smelled of death. Crockett knew this was one of those times that he must have some quick decisive action or maybe end up dead.

The outlaw spoke in a graveled voice, and asks, "Got any money sonny?"

Crockett screamed and ran Jake straight at the outlaw's horse. The outlaw's horse was shocked and reared up in panic and the outlaw fell to the ground with a thud. The outlaw's horse ran up the road about thirty yards and Crockett road after it. Crockett knew he had to get out of range before the outlaw recovered. He caught up with the horse grabbed the reign and galloped up the road and around the next bend. Crockett kept a good pace for at least a mile before he stopped.
He dismounted and unsaddled the other horse. He threw the saddle into the weeds.

Then he looked into the outlaw's saddle bag. He had some jerky and parched corn. He also had a small leather bag filled with gold and silver coins. No weapons were in the Saddlebags. Crockett counted the money and decided this must be blood money taken from the outlaw's victims. There was almost Four Hundred Dollars in gold and silver.

Crockett hurriedly took the money and put it in his saddle bags, and threw the outlaws saddle bags in the weeds on the other side of the trail. Then he got back on Jake and hurried on up the trail leading the saddle-less horse. Crockett was thinking as his heart still raced. What am I to do with all of this money?

Then he realized that he was a hunted man by the law and by an outlaw. Crockett led the horse a few more miles until he came to another little settlement. (Present day Williamson West Virginia established in 1892)

As Crockett slowed down and walked Jake into the little village, a man came out to Crockett.

"Young man, where did you get that horse you are leading?" the man asked excitedly.

Crockett's Long Trip To Kentucky

"Why do you ask?" Crockett answered.

"A devil riding that horse came here and robbed us and beat up some of the folks just the other day," The man answered.

"How much money did he take?" Crockett asked.

By now five or six men joined the first and all recognized the horse that Crockett led. The men talked about the money the bandit took and figured it to be close to Four Hundred Dollars.

Crockett knew in his heart what he must do. He got down and told the people about his encounter with the outlaw and described him to the men. They were shocked that a young fellow like this could have outwitted the devil.

Then Crockett went to the saddle bag and pulled out the little leather sack. Well folks I have recovered your money for you, Crockett said.

The men marveled and cheered when they saw the money as Crockett poured out some gold and silver in his hand. Crockett put the coins back into the little sack and handed it to the man that first came to him.

"Here you go, you fellers will have to decide who gets what," Crockett said.
The men could not believe it. They were so happy. By now the women and children had gathered around. Crockett told them that the outlaw was walking and most likely would be after him.

A Hatfield man spoke up, "Don't worry son we will take care of him if he comes this way."

All the men agreed that they must do away with this devil, when he came back.

"We must reward this fine young man," declared one of the elderly ladies.

"He has restored our wealth and must be rewarded," she sounded the second time.
"God has answered our prayers through this young messenger," another lady

Crockett's Long Trip To Kentucky

said.

Each of the men gave Crockett a five dollar gold piece and the women ran home to gather traveling food for Crockett. A feed bag filled with oats was brought out from a barn, as a reward for Crockett's fine horse.

"That is not necessary," Crockett exclaimed.

"Yes it is, son, go in peace, we must get ready for that varmint that is coming this way," the man said.

"Son can I ask the name of our hero?" a McCoy man asked.

"Well sir I ain't no hero, but my name is David Crockett Whitt," Crockett answered.

"For what happened down the river today, I must give God all the credit for being with me, and delivering me from the hands of the evil man," Crockett said.

Crockett gave the outlaws horse to the people to use as they saw fit. It was probably tied there in town to draw the bad man out in the open.
Crockett rode on down the trail with thirty dollars and saddle bags full of food. He turned Jake sideways and waved to the people. They all cheered and waved. As Crockett rode out of sight the families made plans to be ready for the bad man. The village men planned an ambush and the women hid their wealth and children.

Crockett never heard about what happened, but imagined that the outlaw devil paid his due. Crockett rode along thanking God for his protection and love. Crockett petted Jake and told him he was a good boy. Crockett realized how valuable Jake had been to him.

That night Crockett camped near present day Sprigg, West Virginia. He dined on some good old fried chicken and other leftovers that the good ladies down river gave him.

Crockett wished that Jonas could have seen him today, even though Crockett did give God the credit. The encounter could have very well turned out in tragedy for Crockett, had not the Lord intervened. Jake did not even have a scratch from the

Crockett's Long Trip To Kentucky

encounter. Jesus was Crockett's new best friend!

Crockett felt good about helping the folks down river today. He even felt a little sorry for the outlaw. He wished that he would find Jesus and not come looking for trouble. Most likely the evil minded man will pay his due tomorrow, or maybe already has. Crockett remembered the Bible saying, be sure your sins will find you out. Crockett reckoned that was why he was on the run from the law. Even though he was guilty he knew he was forgiven by the Lord. He felt so alive and did not fear the wilderness he was traveling through. This was some of the most primitive lands still in eastern North America. The woods teemed with wildlife and the trees were mostly virgin timber. This area was isolated just because of where it lay. It was protected by the very mountains that surrounded young David Crockett Whitt

Since Crockett had been traveling up the Tug he has heard a panther scream, and wolves howling! He has seen bear, deer, turkey, squirrels, rabbits, foxes, beavers, river otters, and one big bull elk. He reckoned it would not be too big of a surprise to see a band of painted warriors running around one of the hills. He knew that the wild Indians were out to the west by 1850.

Crockett kept a pretty big fire and Jake close to him during the nights. Crockett would hang the feed bag on Jake and let him enjoy it for a while, then let him graze too many oats is not good for a horse.

Crockett didn't fish or do much other work this evening, other than gathering fire wood. He just sat back and reflected on all that had happened in the last two weeks. He felt real bad about hitting Bill Thompson, but could not take it back. He knew that he was forgiven by God, and that was most important. He knew that folks in Truittville may never forgive him.
Crockett vowed to never let a woman influence him so mightily again. He reckoned women were mostly trouble for men, except maybe a few like his Maw Susannah, or Grand maw Rachel.

Crockett's mind wondered back to the family in Tazewell County. He decided once he got back to Uncle James' he would sit down quietly and tell him the whole blessed story and put himself at his mercy.

It has been a long three years since Jonas and he pulled out for Kentucky. He

Crockett's Long Trip To Kentucky

reckoned he was a new uncle several times by now. He would be glad to see his older brothers and sisters again.

Crockett made one mistake during his travels in the wilderness. He should have been hanging his food up high in a tree. Crockett had his food under his lean to and a hungry bruin got a whiff of it. Crockett awoke with a startle as Jake was raising cane. Crockett jumped up and thinking fast, he grabbed a blazing stick from the fire and waved it and screamed. He scared that poor bear out of two years growth. Crockett understood his situation as for keeping food in camp from then on.

The little valley that the Tug ran through began to close even tighter. There was not many places offering good grazing for Jake, so every time Crockett saw a patch of grass he would let Jake do some munching. One good thing the cliffs offered many rock houses to shelter in at night. One day Crockett stopped at an overhanging cliff for the night and as he cleaned back the leaves he found a pick and shovel. The handles were rotted away and the shovel was mostly rusted away. The pick was in pretty good condition. How in thunder did these things get here, he wondered? He decided to keep the pick.

Crockett always cleared back the leaves before making a bed in one of the many rock houses along the Tug. He drug a black snake out one evening, which gave him and Jake some excitement. Crockett was not too afraid of most snakes long as he knew where they were. He and Jake did have a close call one day on the trail when they happened upon a huge timber rattler. Jake just about threw Crockett off, but managed to get by the deadly viper. Crockett prayed a prayer of thanksgiving and praised the Lord for his protection.

The Tug fork was getting to be a small stream now and Crockett knew it would not be far to his destination. He figured another week or so and he would ride in to Baptist Valley. He would head straight to Uncle James and Aunt Nancy Whitt's house. He knew it well, as it was the old home place of Grand Paw Hezekiah Whitt. He has had a great adventure for the past three weeks. He has tasted hunger and thirst; he has experienced fear and destitution. He also experienced valor and happiness for overcoming many obstacles. The best thing he could think of was the conversion that night on the banks of the Tug. Whatever he had to face, he knew the Lord would be with him. He did not have a Bible, but he craved to study Gods word.

Crockett's Long Trip To Kentucky

Today Crockett passed through what is known today as Wyoming City, West Virginia. It would be about two days ride to the area known today as Paynesville, West Virginia. Another two days he would be in the area known today as Pea patch, West Virginia. About two more days and Jake would carry Crockett through Bear Waller then to Harmon, then to what is now called the town of Bandy. A half days ride from Bandy through the area known as Bust Head and another mile he will be home again. Crockett figured about the 15th or 16th of July 1850 he would be there.

After another grueling week in the wilderness of upper Tug Fork, Crockett begins to see more cabins and more people. Crockett guides Jake up a feeder branch and crosses over into the water shed of the Clinch River. Today he starts out near present day Bandy, Virginia. He worked his way down the trail toward Indian Creek and to his destination.

Crockett is anxious to get to the James Whitt house, yet he has some dread also. He is going to do as he planned, and that is to get Uncle James off to himself and tell him the whole story of why he is here. He will do whatever it takes, either to stay with James Whitt, or move on if he is shunned. Crockett knows in his heart that he is forgiven by the Lord, and the Lord will be with him. He is not sure what James will say or do, but feels that James will welcome him.

Finally Jake carried Crockett to Indian Creek, on the 16th day of July 1850. In just a short ride he would be there. Crockett's heart was racing a bit, knowing he would be with family in a short while. He traveled up the Kentucky Turnpike into Baptist Valley. Crockett saw the turn off up Green mountain road and turned Jake. Jake seems to know this place also. There on the little rise on the right is the old Hezekiah Whitt house. Now it is the James Whitt house and there on the porch is a lady sitting there doing something.

Crockett gets closer and recognizes her as Nancy Whitt his aunt. She is stringing new green beans.

Crockett rode Jake right up to the porch and with a wide smile says, "Hello there Aunt Nancy."

"Oh my gracious, is that you David Crockett?" Nancy asked.

Crockett's Long Trip To Kentucky

"Yes ma-um it is me," Crockett said.

"How in thunder did you get here?" Nancy asked.

"Jake brought me," Crockett said with a laugh.

"Well get up here and let me hug you," Nancy said.

Crockett got off Jake and tied him to a porch support, and walked around to come up on the porch.

"My goodness Crockett you are so tall," Nancy said in amazement.

"Yes ma-um, reckon I have grown up a might," Crockett said.

Nancy gave Crockett a good welcome hug, and Crockett felt a little more at ease.

"Where is Uncle James, is he about today?" Crockett asked.

"He is out in the barn I think; want me to ring the bell?" Nancy asked.
"No Ma-um I would rather surprise him, I will take Jake to the barn and see to his needs and surprise Uncle James," Crockett said.

Uncle James was working on repairing a single tree when Crockett walked in through the barn door. James looked up in astonishment as he recognized Crockett.

"Well I be Crockett, you are so tall," James said.

"Son is everything alright, is Jonas with you?" James asked.

"No sir just me and Jake, I need to talk to you Uncle James," Crockett said.

James pointed to a bench over to one side, and said," Let's go and sit over there and you can tell me all about it."
"Let me get Jake took care of first, can Jake have some oats Uncle James?" Crockett asked.

Crockett's Long Trip To Kentucky

"Sure can, I will fill a feed bag while you unsaddle him," James said.

"This place sure looks good to me," Crockett said as he took off the saddle and all the gear that was tied on it.

James noticed the rusted pick, but didn't say anything about it. With Jake cared for, James and Crockett sat down together on the bench.

"Uncle James, I don't know hardly where to begin, I am so ashamed of what I done, but I know that God has forgiven me," Crockett affirmed.

James sits there waiting patiently.

"Well Crockett just start at the beginning, and tell me, I am your family and you can confide in me," James said.

"Uncle James it all started right after we got to Kentucky, Paws new wife Millie has a little sister, and I fell for her," Crockett said.

James nodded for Crockett to go on.

"Well sir she flirted with me, but decided to marry Bill Thompson," Crockett said.

"I was filled with rage and wanted to give Bill a good whipping, but I figured I weren't man enough yet," Crockett continued.

"What happened next?" James asked.

"Well sir, a reasoned that if I softened him up a might, I could handle him, so I plotted out a quick plan, I knew that Bill always took care of the Truitt horses every evening about dark, so I got myself a club and hid in the barn," Crockett continued..

James sits with his mouth opened, and listens.

"When Bill came in and walked into a stall, I gave him a good lick, and got ready to fight, but He fell to the floor dead," Crockett said with tears welling up in his

Crockett's Long Trip To Kentucky

gray eyes.

"What happened next?" James asked.

"I panicked and ran for Paw, and paw was coming toward the barn when I saw him," Crockett said.

"What did Jonas tell you to do?" James asked.

"Paw was hurt and shocked, but he told me to saddle up Jake and get out of Kentucky real quick, he gave me twenty dollars and me and Jake slipped out of Truittville," Crockett stated.

"Paw told me I would get hung if I stayed around and to come to you, never to write or let anybody know where I was," Crockett added.

James was in shock at the story Crockett told him.

"Uncle James I never set out to kill poor old Bill, I just wanted to do some whipping for taking my girl," Crockett said.

"Bill was a good feller except for marring Mary Elizabeth, Uncle James I prayed on the trail and have accepted Jesus as my personal Savior, and I know He has forgiven me," Crockett said.

"I hope in time Paw, and you can also forgive me," Crockett pleaded.

James took out his pipe and filled it while he pondered on the situation. He lit the pipe and gave it a puff or two. James looked at Crockett really intently.

"Son, do you want to stay here and work for me for room and board?" James asked.

"I was hoping to do just that Sir," Crockett answered.

"Well alright we will try this out, I don't want you to tell another soul of what you just told me not even Nancy, and do you understand Crockett?" James asked.

"Yes sir, I understand completely," Crockett answered.

Crockett's Long Trip To Kentucky

"Alright son you are welcome here, and I will protect you the very best I can," James said.

"If for some reason you don't hold up your bargain, or cause us any trouble I will send you packing, understand?" James asked.

"Yes Sir, I understand, you will not have any trouble out of me Uncle James," Crockett answered.

"Alright Son we will not talk of it again, just consider yourself as my adopted son and me as your adopted Paw," James said.

Crockett reached out to shake his hand, but James grabbed him and gave him a big hug. Crockett felt a big burden lift from his shoulders, as he realized James has forgiven him.

"I have one question Crockett, where did you get that old rusted pick?" James asked.

"I cleared out under a rock house to spend the night and found it and a rusted away shovel," Crockett said.

"Handles rotted away?" James asked.

"The handles, and most of the shovel," replied Crockett.

"Reckon who might have left them there in the wilderness?" Asked Crockett?

"Only one name comes to mind, and that would be just a big guess," replied James.

"Who was that Uncle James?" Crockett asked.

"There is a story been floating round these parts since I was a young-un, and that feller's name was Jonathan Swift, he supposedly had a silver mine here in the mountains someplace," James exclaimed.

"That might be his pick," Crockett responded.

Crockett's Long Trip To Kentucky

"Could very well be, that is the only answer for how a pick and shovel ended up out there in the wilderness," James said.

"What happened to that Swift feller Uncle James?" Crockett asked.

"The story was that he dug out a fine cache of silver, smelted it into English Coins and went back east, then he went blind and never could get back to the silver he hid so well," answered James.
"I reckon that stuff might be Jonathan Swift's old pick and shovel I found," Crockett said.

"Was there anything else that might make you think a silver mine might be around?" James asked.

"Not a thing Uncle James, but I wasn't looking for none neither," Crockett responded.

Crockett made it back to Tazewell County after many years in Kentucky. He was back just in time to be caught up in the Great Civil War.

Crockett's Long Trip To Kentucky

About The Author

Colonel Whitt was born and raised in Tazewell County VA. He has resided in Flatwoods KY since 1970.

The Colonel is a researcher, genealogist, and author of 12 books.

His books are mostly historic by nature but he adds conversations and emotions to the facts to make the books really interesting. He calls his books Historic-Fiction where all is based on truth and all the names, dates, places, and events are true.

The Colonel is a member of the Sons of the American Revolution, The Sons of Confederate Veterans and a Kentucky Colonel. He wears his uniform of the Confederate Colonel to honor all the men and women that struggled against the Union during the War of Northern Aggression. Colonel Whitt has been recognized by the Kentucky Senate on two occasions for his achievements in historic research and writing ability and also a member of Biltmore's Who's Who.

Dahnmon Whitt grew up in Raven, VA, and attended Richlands High School. In his younger days he fished, played games with friends, and was a Boy Scout for several years. He was raised in a Christian home and has tried to be the man his dog thinks he is. He served in the U.S. Navy from 1964 to 1968. He learned the craft of Sheet Metal Work and earned a living until December 2003. Dahnmon has always wanted to know his place and where he came from so in 1999 he purchased his first computer. Doing genealogy he made so many discovers including his connections in KY. And back to Ireland, Scotland, and to the American Indians as he is the GGGG Grandson of Chief Cornstalk the Shawnee War Chief.

To see the Colonel Whitt's work please go to: http://dahnmonwhittfamily.com/

E-mail c-dahnmon@roadrunner.com

Address is post office box 831

Flatwoods, KY 41139

Phone 606 836 7997 or

Cell 606 571 1820

www.ingramcontent.com/pod-product-compliance
Lightning Source LLC
Chambersburg PA
CBHW051045160426
43193CB00010B/1069